# ELVIRA LANTENHAMMER

## Color Siteplan

HIRMER

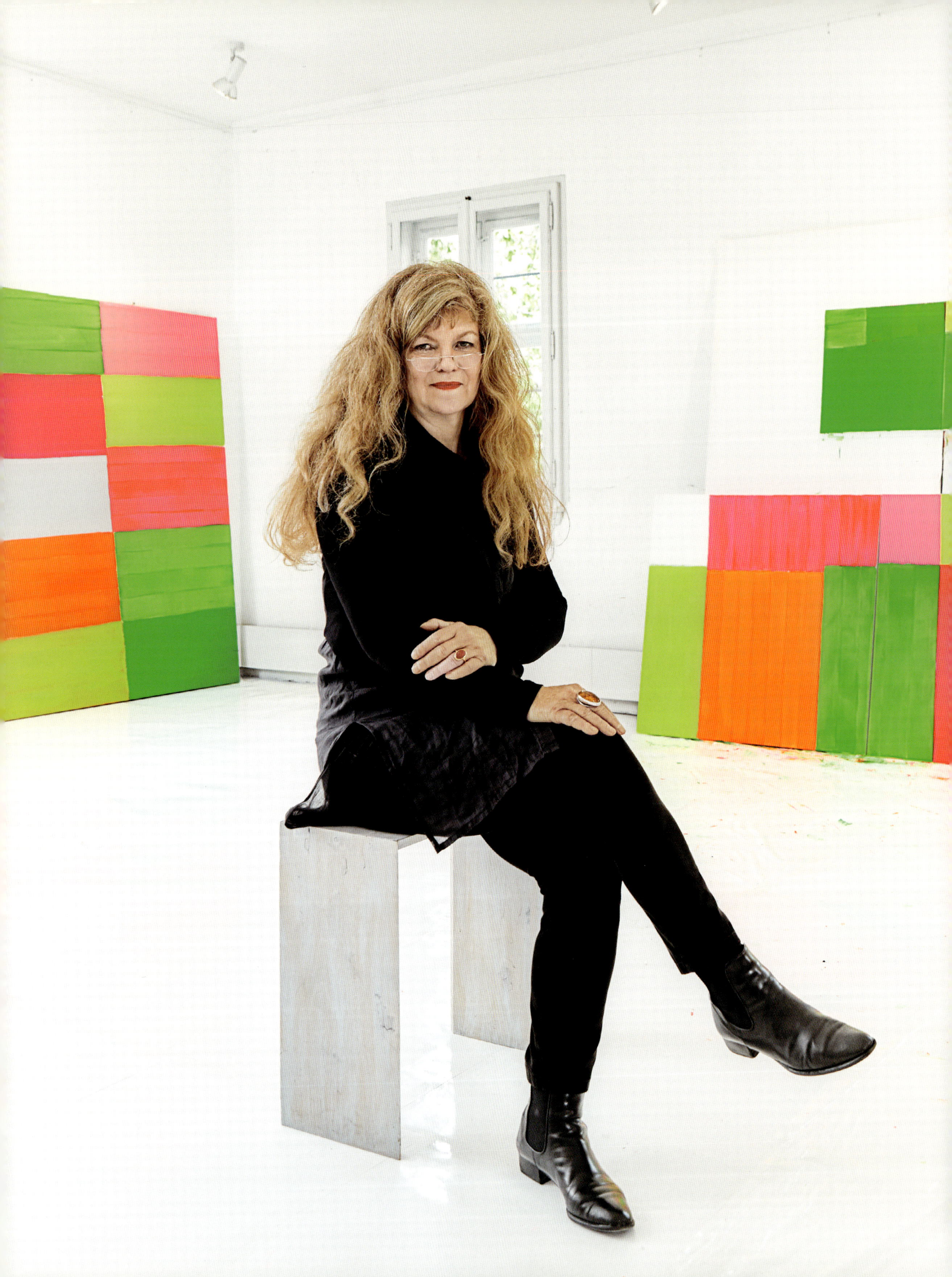

# ELVIRA LANTENHAMMER
## Color Siteplan

If you can turn off the mind
and look only with the eyes,
ultimately everything becomes abstract.

Ellsworth Kelly

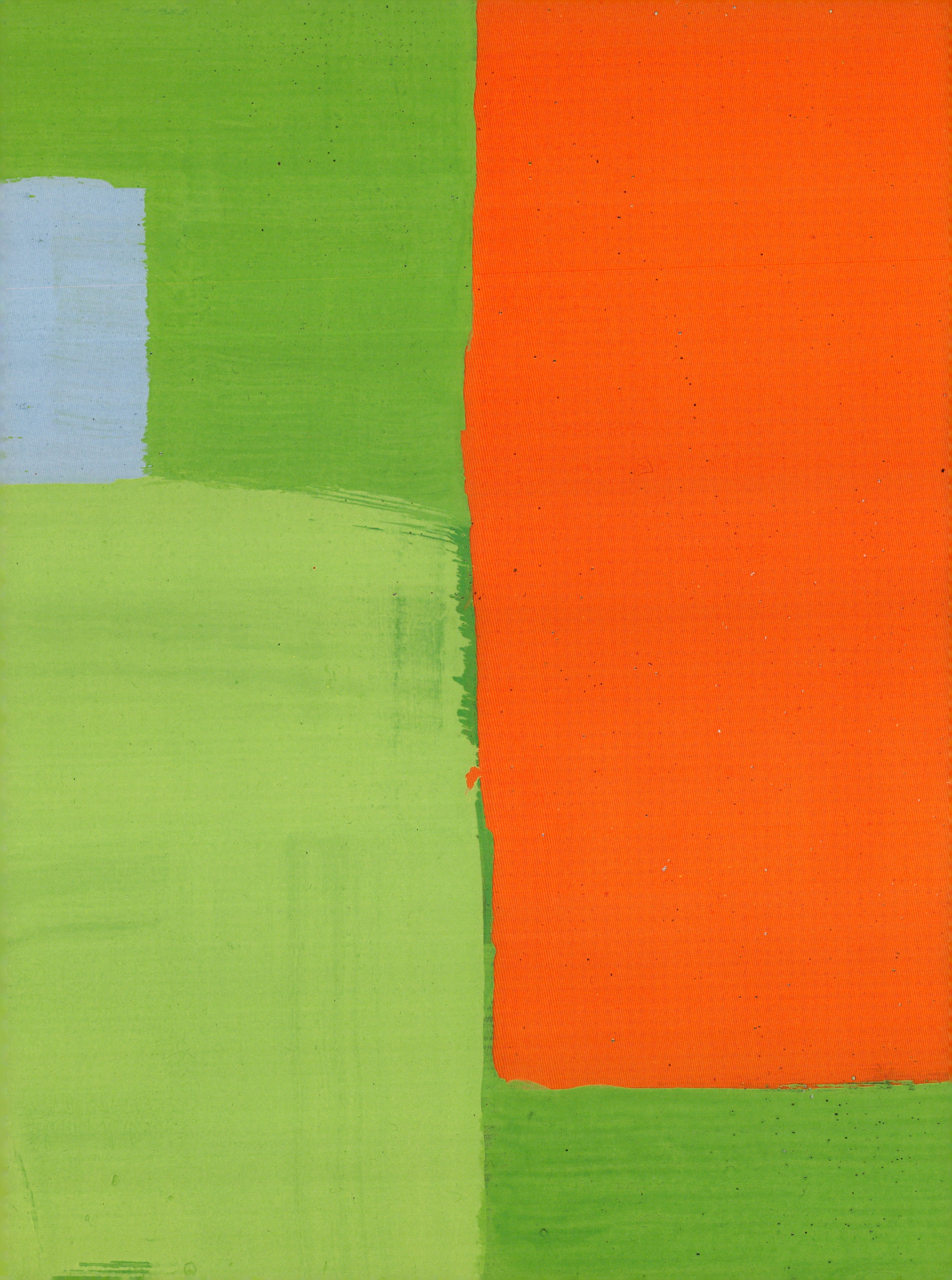

# Inhalt
# Content

# Sensible Nachbarschaften
## Elvira Lantenhammers Farbfeldmalerei

Elvira Lantenhammers Bilder sind Farbereignisse. Seit ihrem Kunststudium in München in den 1980er-Jahren untersucht die zuvor als Restauratorin ausgebildete und daher immer auch an der Farbmaterie und der handwerklichen Anwendung der Farbe interessierte Malerin die Wirkung von Farben: fein abgestimmt oder in kühnen Komplementärkontrasten, in Schichten übereinander aufgetragen oder so durchlässig, dass die helle Grundierung hindurchschimmert, anfangs auch von Ritzungen aufgebrochen. Jedes der Bilder ist ein sinnliches Erlebnis für sich, das ganz wesentlich auf Farbsensitivität beruht.

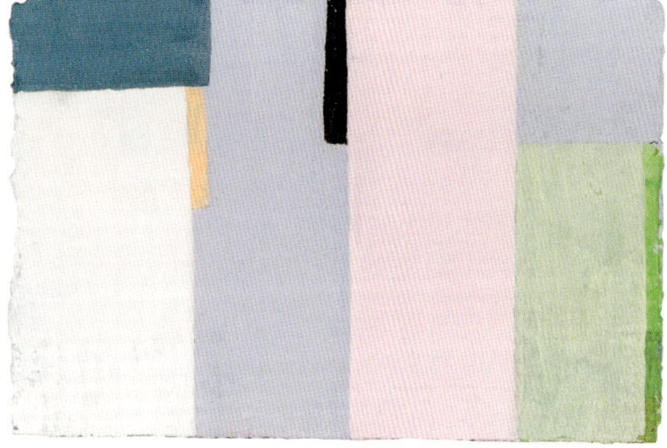

Siteplan Sadiq's House, 2017
Pigment | Acrylics | Handmade paper
7.4 x 11.4 in. | 19 x 29 cm

Lantenhammer bewegt sich damit in einer Tradition der Farbfeldmalerei, wie sie vor allem nach dem Zweiten Weltkrieg in den USA begründet und kultiviert wurde: Künstler wie Barnett Newman, Mark Rothko oder Clyfford Still, die aus dem Abstrakten Expressionismus hervorgegangen waren, machten die Farbe zum Hauptakteur ihrer Bilder. Die Farbwahl und ihr Auftrag erfolgte im Unterschied etwa zu Josef Albers' systematischen Farbuntersuchungen intuitiv, in einem Erspüren der Farbwirkungen und ihres Zusammenspiels.

# Sensitive Neighborhoods
## Elvira Lantenhammer's Color field painting

Elvira Lantenhammer's pictures are color events. Since her art studies in Munich in the 1980s, the painter, who had previously trained as a restorer and was therefore always interested in the matter of color and the manual application of color, has been investigat-ing the effect of colors: finely tuned or in bold complementary contrasts, applied on top of one another in layers or so permeable that the light primer shimmers through, initially also broken open by engravings. Each of the pictures is a sensual experience in its own right, which is essentially based on color sensitivity. Lantenhammer thus moves in a tradition of color field painting as it was founded and cultivated in the USA, especially after the Second World War: artists such as Barnett Newman, Mark Rothko, and Clyfford Still, who emerged from Abstract Expressionism, made color the main protagonist of their pictures. In contrast to Josef Albers' systematic investigations of color, the choice of color and its application were intuitive, in a sense of the effects of color and their interplay.

In the course of her more than thirty years of work, Lantenhammer has followed her very own path of color field painting, which is characterized in particular

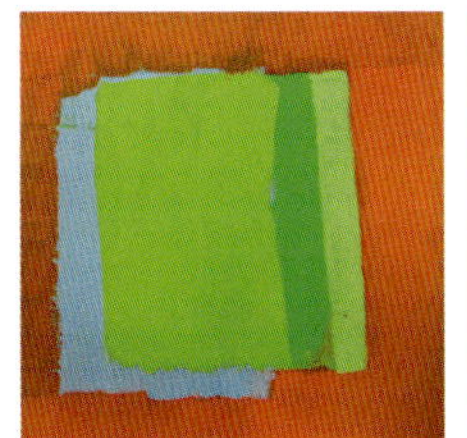
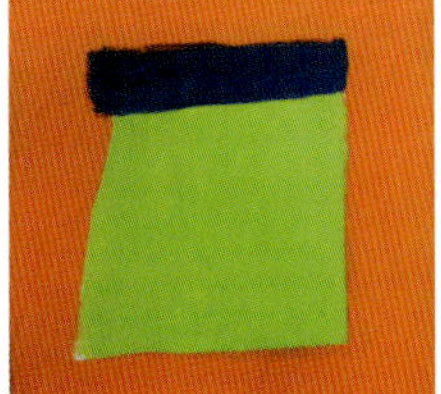
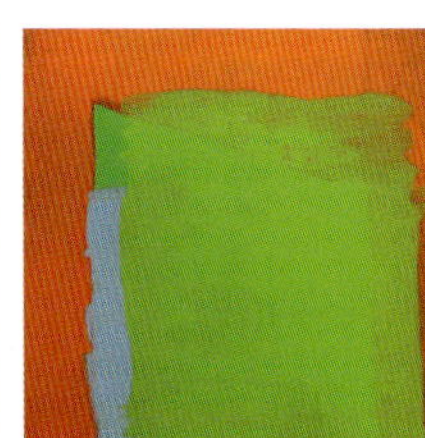

Place for Spring 1-3, 2013
Pigment | Egg tempera | Wood
each 7.9 x 7.9 in. | 20 x 20 cm

In ihrem mittlerweile mehr als dreißigjährigen Schaffen ist Lantenhammer ihrem ganz eigenen Weg der Farbfeldmalerei gefolgt, der insbesondere von ihrer Beschäftigung mit östlicher Philosophie und dem Zen-Buddhismus geprägt ist. Am vorläufigen Endpunkt dieser Entdeckungsreise in ein achtsames, sensitives Farbempfinden steht nicht zufällig ihre Reise nach Japan im Jahr 2017 und die daraus entstandene Serie der „Japanese Siteplans". Der hier entwickelte Farbklang aus Weiß und aus rosa, gelben und grünen Leuchtfarben spiegelt das innere Leuchten, das die Reise in das Sehnsuchtsland ausgelöst hatte; der regelmäßig streichende Farbauftrag des Flachpinsels verrät etwas von der meditativen Haltung beim Malen – vergleichbar mit dem Harken eines japanischen Steingartens und den dabei entstehenden Spuren.

Elvira Lantenhammer reiht diese Bilderserie in ihre „Lagepläne" („siteplans") ein – ein Begriff, den sie 1996 entwickelt hat und unter den alle abstrakten Werke sich seitdem subsummieren. Ein zentraler Begriff also, den es sich lohnt, näher zu beleuchten. Zunächst einmal betont das Wort „Lageplan" die Flächigkeit der Bilder; statt eine dreidimensionale Realität auf zweidimensionaler Fläche vorzuspiegeln, wie die traditionelle Malerei es sich Jahrhunderte lang zum Ziel gesetzt hatte, bannt der Lageplan reale Gegebenheiten von vornherein in die Fläche. Die Topographie einer Landschaft oder einer Stadt wird auf einer Landkarte, in einem Lageplan, in symbolhaften Zeichen visualisiert: Rosa Vierecke stehen für Bebauung, grüne Flächen für Parks, blaue Linien für Flüsse. Die Landschaften werden dafür genau vermessen, der Plan ist eine exakte Übersetzung der realen Gegebenheiten in die Fläche. Insofern ist der Begriff des „Lageplans" bei Lantenhammer natürlich im übertragenen Sinn zu verstehen. Ihr geht es um die Wirkung eines Ortes; nicht um sein reales Dasein, sondern darum, was er für das innere Erleben bedeutet. Weniger das Vermessen als das Erspüren.

by her preoccupation with Eastern philosophy and Zen Buddhism. It is no coincidence that her journey to Japan in 2017 and the resulting series of "Japanese Siteplans" are, for now, at the end of this voyage of discovery into an attentive, sensitive perception of color. The color tone developed here, consisting of white, of pink, yellow and green luminous colors, reflects the inner glow that triggered the journey to the land of longing; the regularly stroking application of paint by the flat brush reveals something of the meditative attitude when painting – comparable to the raking of a Japanese rock garden and the traces that are left behind as a result.

Elvira Lantenhammer places this series of paintings in her "siteplans" – a term that she developed in 1996 and under which all abstract works have subsumed ever since. A central concept, therefore, that is worth taking a closer look at. First of all, the word "siteplan" emphasizes the flatness of the pictures; instead of simulating a three-dimensional reality on a two-dimensional surface, as traditional painting had set itself the goal for centuries, the siteplan captures real conditions onto the surface from the outset. The topography of a landscape or a city is visualized on a map, in a siteplan, in symbolic signs: pink squares stand for buildings, green areas for parks, blue lines for rivers. The landscapes are measured exactly, the plan is an exact translation of the real conditions onto the surface. In this respect, the Lantenhammer's term "siteplan" is to be understood in a figurative sense. She is concerned with the effect of a place; not with its real existence, but with what it means for the inner experience. Less of the measuring than of the feeling.

These places can be places of spirit or mythology ("Lageplan Apokalypse" or "Atlantis") – or concrete cities,

Kakemono -
Japanese Siteplan, 2017
Acrylics | Pigment | Shōji-paper
472.4 x 39.4 in | 1200 x 100 cm

Diese Orte können Orte des Geistes oder der Mythologie sein („Lageplan Apokalypse" oder „Atlantis") – oder konkrete Städte, Dörfer, Länder – wie etwa in den Lageplänen zu Rom, zu Würzburg, zu Aschaffenburg in den 1990er-Jahren, zu Bremerhaven, Bulgarien, Virginia oder eben Japan in den letzten Werkserien. Gelegentlich spiegeln Lantenhammers Werke Formen wider, die einen Ort besonders prägen, am deutlichsten vielleicht in den Lageplänen zu ihrer Heimatstadt Altötting, in denen die Fixpunkte der Kindheit – Elternhaus, Schule, Gnadenkapelle, verbunden durch Plätze und Wege – sich zu einer persönlichen Topografie der Erinnerung zusammenfügen. In den Lageplänen „Bremerhaven" greift Lantenhammer die Form der Hafenbecken auf.

Meist jedoch sind es allein die Farbklänge und ihr Miteinander in einem fein austarierten Gefüge von Farbflächen, die die emotionalen und energetischen Qualitäten eines Ortes oder eines Landes spürbar machen. So hat jeder Ort, jedes Land, das Elvira Lantenhammer in den letzten Jahren häufig im Rahmen von Künstlerstipendien bereist hat, einen eigenen Klang: Bremerhaven ist orange, grün, schwarz und weiß, Bulgarien grün, rot, schwarz und weiß, Virginia rosa, gelb, grün, grau, schwarz und weiß. Am Beispiel der „Virginian Siteplans" erklärt Elvira Lantenhammer im Interview mit Wolfgang Hülsen selbst, wie die einzelnen Farben zum Bedeutungsträger werden: Gelb kann für die Sonne stehen, Grün für die üppige

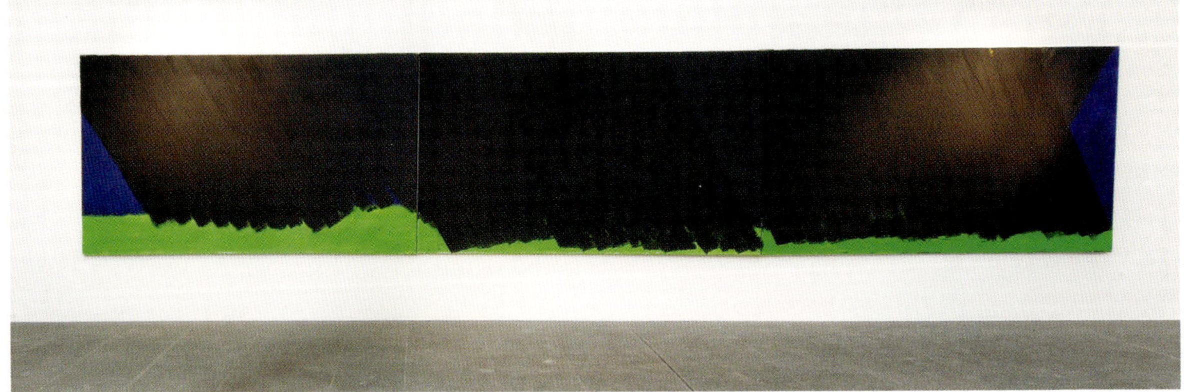

Apocalypse Triptych, 2010
Pigment | Acrylics | Canvas
55.1 x 236.1 in. | 140 x 600 cm

villages, countries – such as in the siteplans of Rome, Würzburg, Aschaffenburg in the 1990s, Bremerhaven, Bulgaria, Virginia or Japan in the last series of works. Occasionally, Lantenhammer's works reflect forms that particularly shape a place, perhaps most clearly in the siteplans of her hometown Altötting, in which the fixed points of childhood – parental home, school, Chapel of Grace, connected by places and paths – come together to form a personal topography of memory. In the "Bremerhaven" siteplans, Lantenhammer takes up the shape of the harbor basins.

Usually, however, it is only the color tones and their coexistence in a finely balanced structure of colored surfaces that make the emotional and energetic qualities of a place or a country perceptible. Thus every place, every country, which Elvira Lantenhammer has visited in recent years, frequently within the framework of artist scholarships, has its own sound: Bremerhaven is orange, green, black, and white, Bulgaria green, red, black, and white, Virginia pink, yellow, green, grey, black, and white. Using the "Virginian Siteplans" as an example, Elvira Lantenhammer explains in an interview with Wolfgang Hülsen how the individual colors become carriers of meaning: yellow can stand for the sun, green for lush nature, pink for the more childlike and cheerful

Natur, Rosa für die kindlich-heitere Seite der amerikanischen Mentalität, Schwarz aber auch für die gesellschaftlichen Brüche und Abgründe.

Schwarz und Weiß als Träger von Dunkelheit und Licht spielen in all diesen Serien eine Rolle – erst in Japan wird das Schwarz ganz durch das Licht verdrängt. Trotz des immer gleichen Farbklangs innerhalb einer Serie variiert der Farbeindruck insgesamt jedoch stark: Je nach Gewichtung der einzelnen Farbe, des Anteils an Schwarz und Weiß werden unterschiedliche Qualitäten fühlbar, je nach Form der Farbflächen – breit gelagert, steil vertikal, ruhend im Quadrat – kann der Eindruck von Harmonie oder Disharmonie, von Ausgewogenheit oder einem Ringen der Farben um die Vorherrschaft entstehen. Die Spielarten des Farbauftrags, durchlässig oder opak, lasierend oder in Schichtungen, mit Überlappungen der Farbfelder an den Rändern oder auch Stellen, an denen die weiße Grundierung durchscheint, fordern den Betrachter zu genauem und lustvollem Sehen auf.

So bietet das Prinzip „Lageplan" eine unendliche Vielzahl an Möglichkeiten, die Elvira Lantenhammer in der Tiefe und in der Breite auslotet. Bilder können durch Ansetzen einer oder mehrerer weiterer Leinwände zu wandfüllenden Panoramen erweitert werden; einzelne Farbformen können herausgelöst, aus dem Büttenpapier herausgerissen und als „Plätze" für sich stehen oder neu arrangiert werden. Schließlich hat Lantenhammer in Japan, inspiriert von den japanischen Ka-

side of the American mentality, black, however, also for the social ruptures and abysses.

Black and white as carriers of darkness and light play a role in all these series – it is only in Japan that black is completely replaced by light alone. Depending on the weighting of the individual colors and the proportion of black and white, different qualities can be felt. Depending on the shape of the color surfaces – broadly supported, steeply vertical, resting in the square – the impression of harmony or disharmony, of balance or a struggle of colors for supremacy can arise. The variations of the color application, permeable or opaque, glazed or in layers, with overlaps of the color fields at the edges or also places where the white primer shines through, challenge the viewer to exact and pleasurable seeing.

Thus, the principle of "siteplan" offers an infinite number of possibilities, which Elvira Lantenhammer explores in depth and width. Pictures can be extended by adding one or more further canvases to form panoramas covering the entire wall; individual color forms can be detached, torn out of the laid paper and used as "places" for themselves or rearranged. Finally, in Japan, Lantenhammer, inspired by the Japanese Kakemonos, has created a twelve meters long scroll painting that, depend-ing on how far it is rolled out and where it is viewed, always offers new visual impressions. When rolled

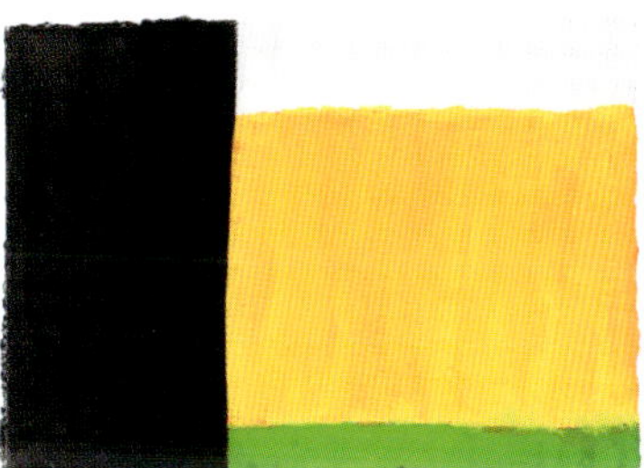

Virginian Siteplan 1-3, 2015
Egg tempera | Pigment |
Handmade paper
each 9.8 x 13.3 in. | 25 x 34 cm

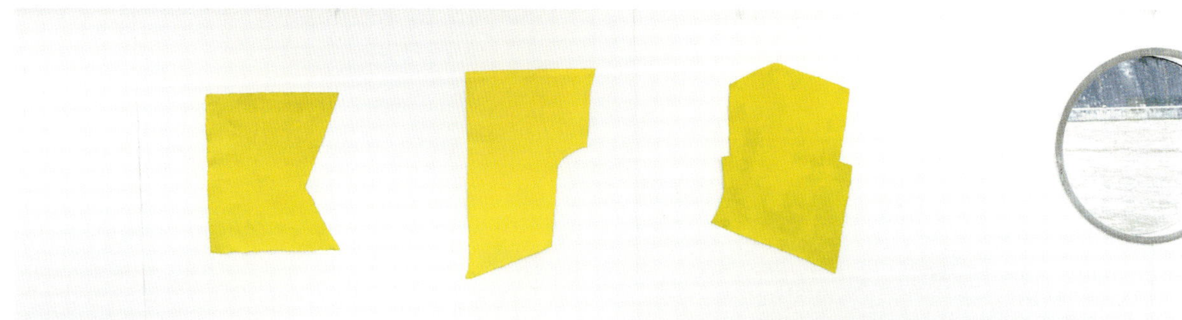

Siteplan Barn Complex 1-3, 2015
Eggtempera | Pigment | Handmade paper
each 39.4 x 26.8 in. | 100 x 68 cm

kemonos, ein zwölf Meter langes Rollbild erschaffen, das je nachdem, wie weit es ausgerollt und an welcher Stelle es betrachtet wird, immer neue Seheindrücke bietet. Aufgerollt kann ein solches Bild auch als Skulptur im Raum stehen. Mit leuchtend blauen und gelben Farbstreifen über Fußboden und Wände im Rahmen einer Kunstaktion im Bahnhof Münnerstadt wagte sich Lantenhammer 2018 schließlich auch in den Bereich der Rauminstallation.

Der „Lageplan" also ist ein Aktionsraster, das sich durch Offenheit auszeichnet und den Farben neue Räume erobert. Entscheidend ist dabei immer wieder die wechselseitige Wirkung der Farben innerhalb dessen, was Lantenhammer selbst das „Gefüge" nennt: das Nebeneinander und Ineinandergreifen von verschiedenen farbigen Flächen. Für die Malerin bieten sich hier immer neue Herausforderungen – und auch für den Betrachter, dem jedes Bild eine überraschende, seine Farbsensitivität berührende Seherfahrung bedeutet. So tritt die Farbe als Elementarkraft aller Malerei ganz in ihr Recht ein.

Henrike Holsing

up, such a picture can also stand in space as a sculpture. Lantenhammer finally ventured into the field of spatial installation in 2018 with bright blue and yellow colored stripes over the floor and walls as part of an art action at Münnerstadt station.

So the "siteplan" is an action grid that is characterized by openness and conquers new spaces with its colors. The reciprocal effect of the colors within what Lantenhammer herself calls the "structure" is decisive: the juxtaposition and interlocking of different colored surfaces. For the painter there are always new challenges – and also for the observer, for whom each picture means a surprising visual experience touching his color sensitivity. Thus color, as the elementary force of all painting, has come fully into its own right.

Henrike Holsing

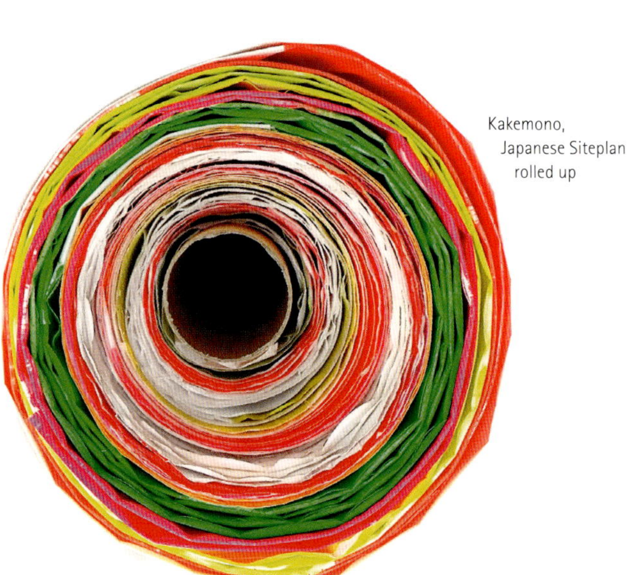

Kakemono,
Japanese Siteplan
rolled up

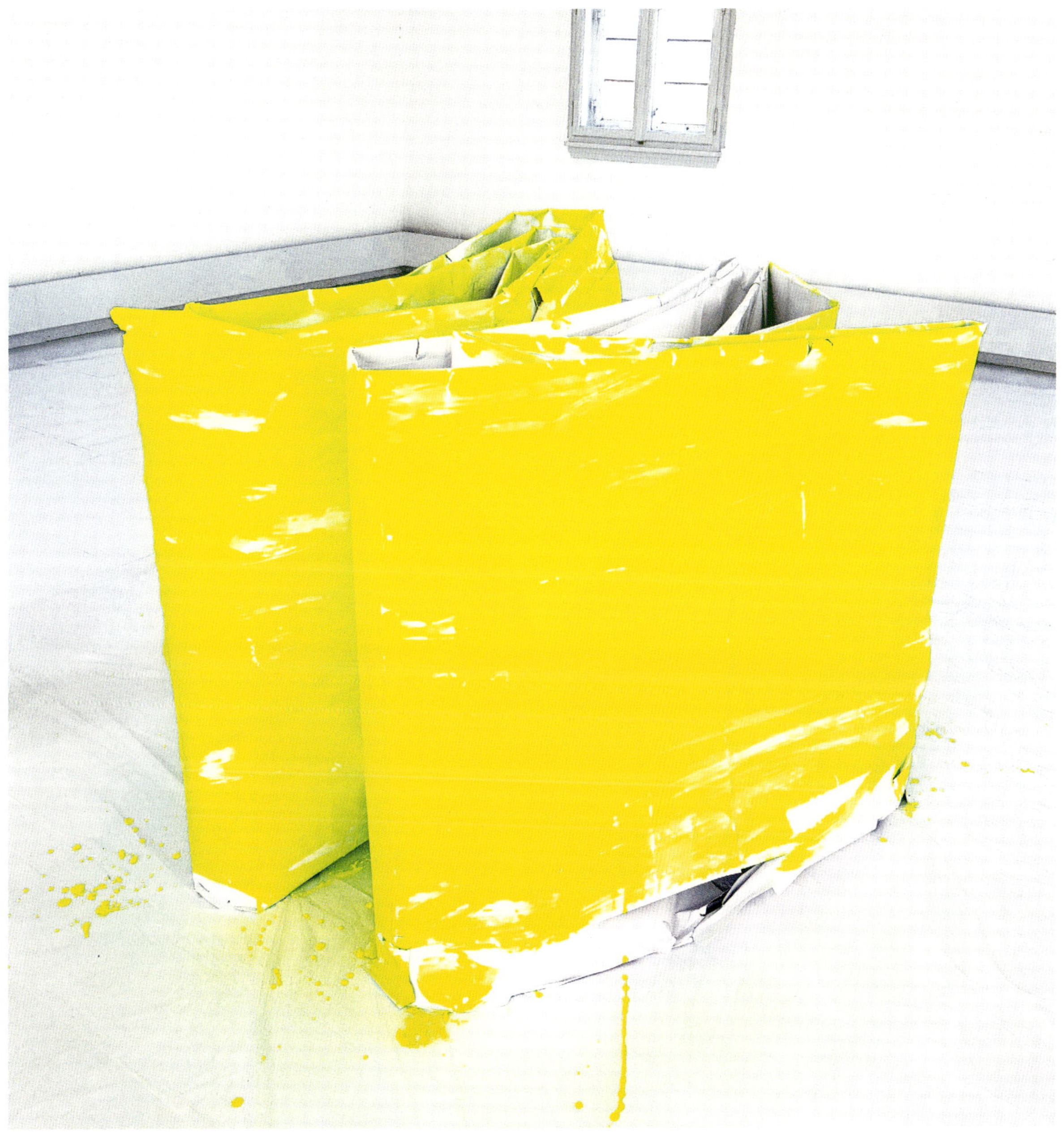

Folding Map | Studio

| Gefüge | Structure |
|---|---|
| Ränder | edges |
| Nachbarschaft | neighborhood |
| Zusammenstoßen | to collide |
| Verschränkung | entanglement |
| Berührung | touch |
| Abtrennen | to cut off |
| Sich treffen | to meet |
| Ausschnitt | section |

Kakemono
Japanese Siteplan, 2017
Acrylics | Pigment | Shōji-paper
7.9 x 7.9 in. | 20 x 20 cm

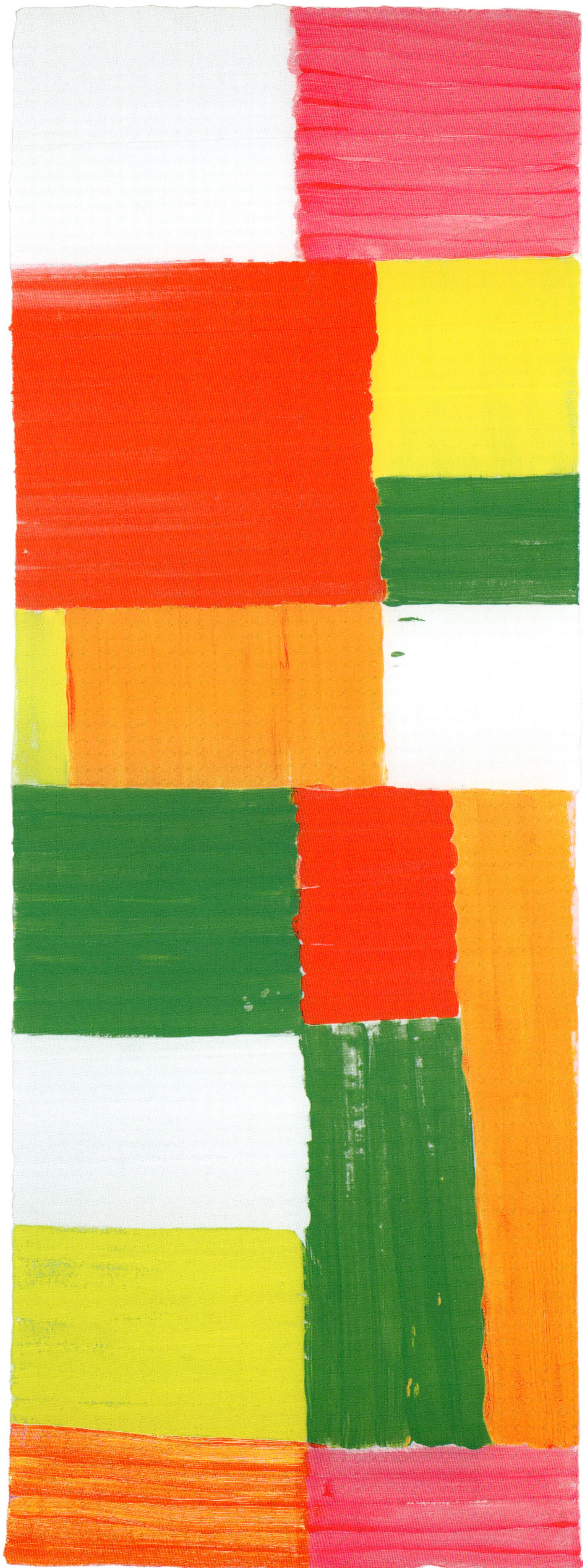

Kakemono
Japanese Siteplan, 2017
Acrylics | Pigment | Shōji-paper
47.2 x 17.7 in. | 120 x 45 cm

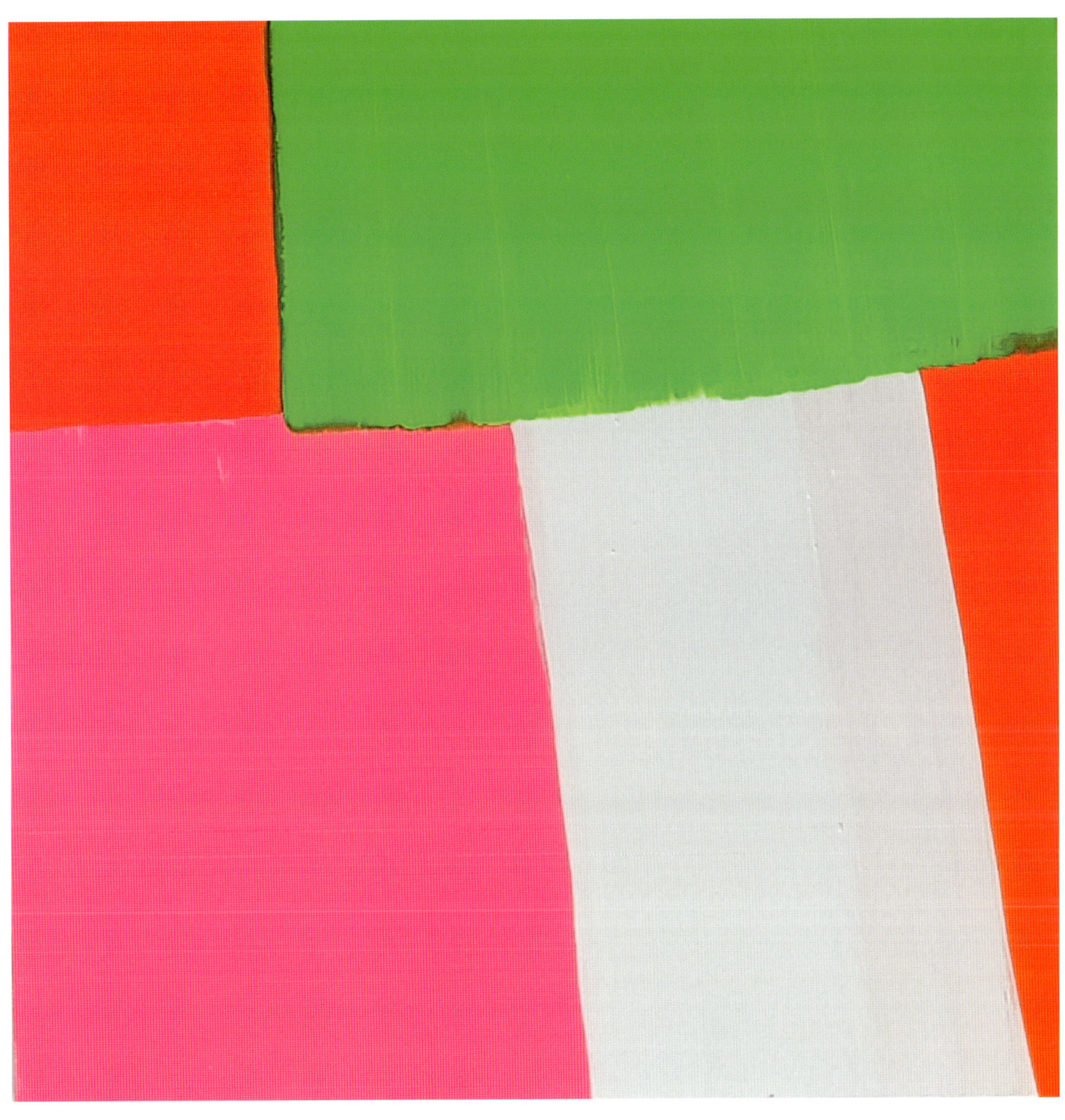

Japanese Siteplan, 2017
Acrylics | Pigment | Canvas
39.4 x 39.4 in. | 100 x 100 cm

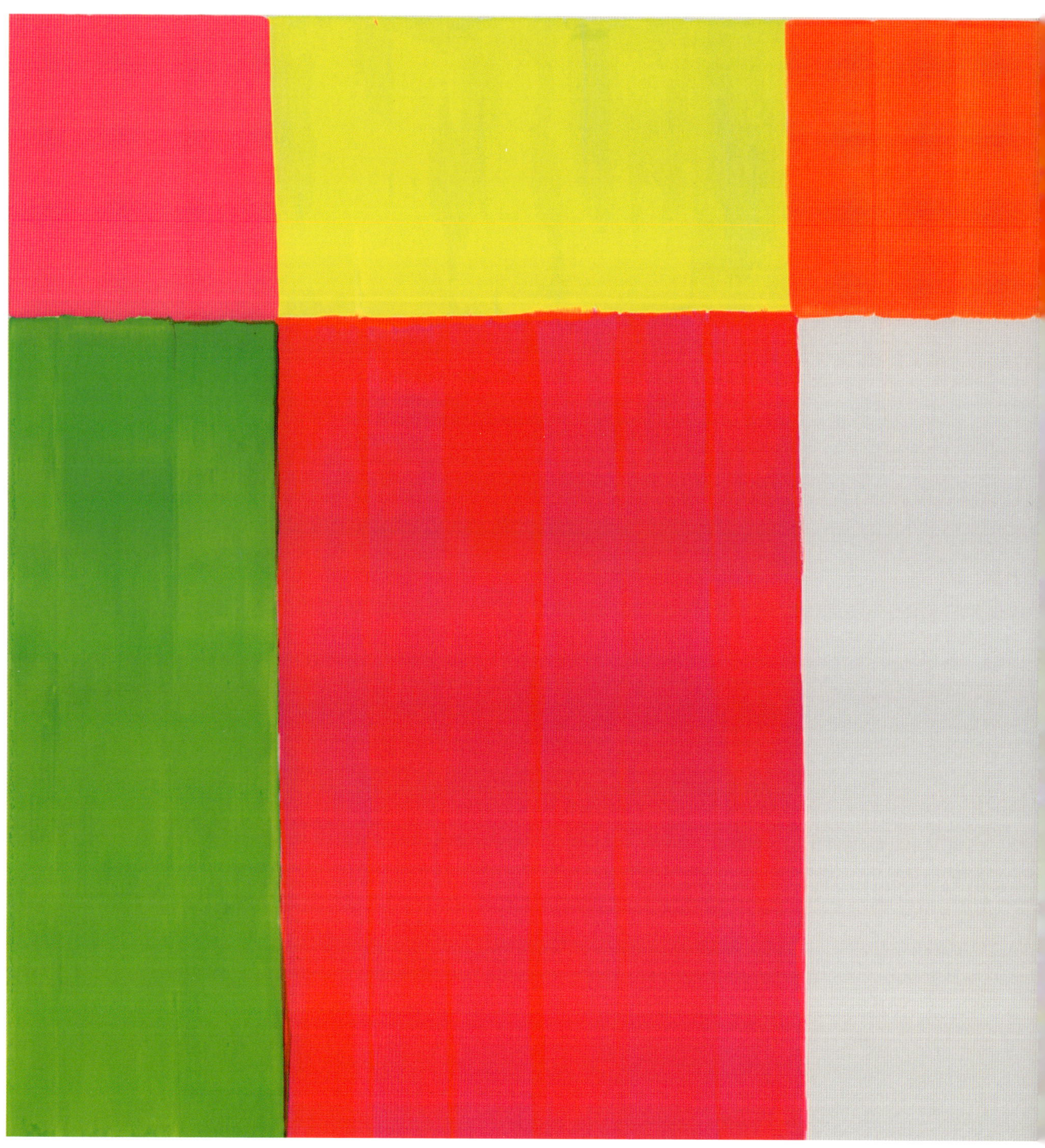

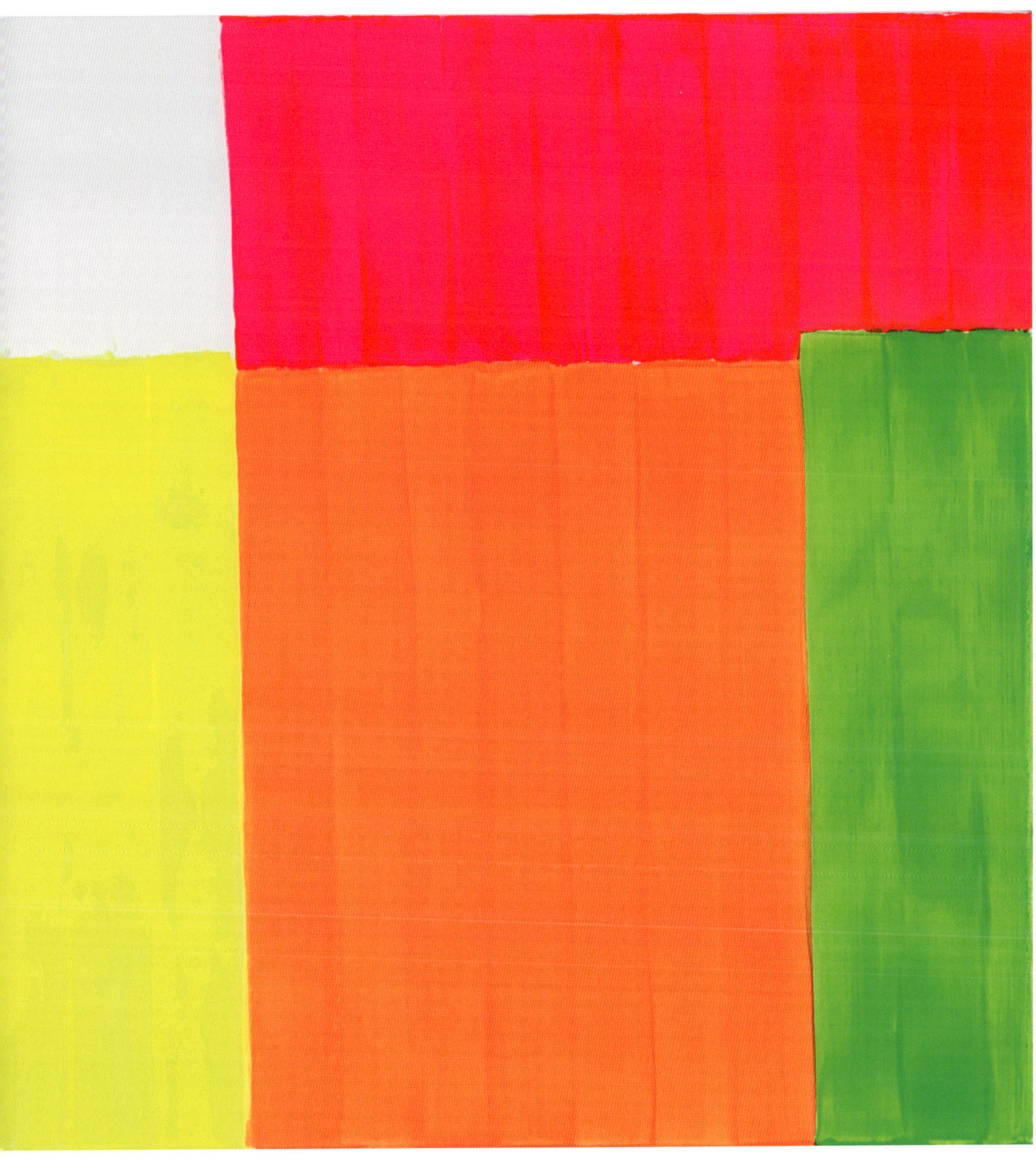

Japanese Siteplan, 2017
Diptych
Acrylics | Pigment | Canvas
39.4 x 78.7 in. | 100 x 200 cm

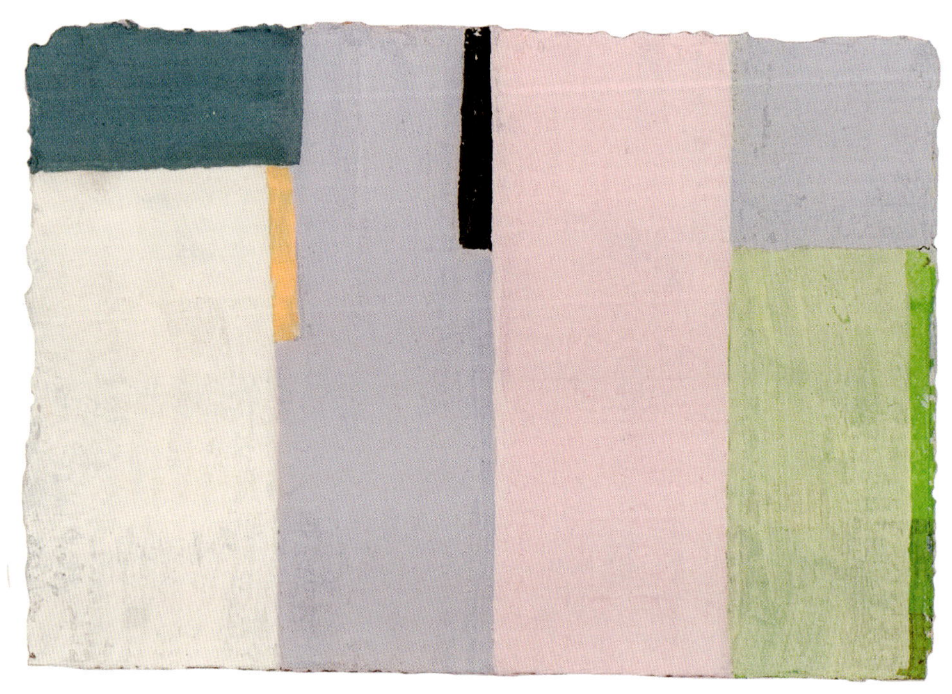

Siteplan Sadiq's House, 2017
Acrylics | Pigment | Handmade paper
7.4 x 11.4 in. | 19 x 29 cm

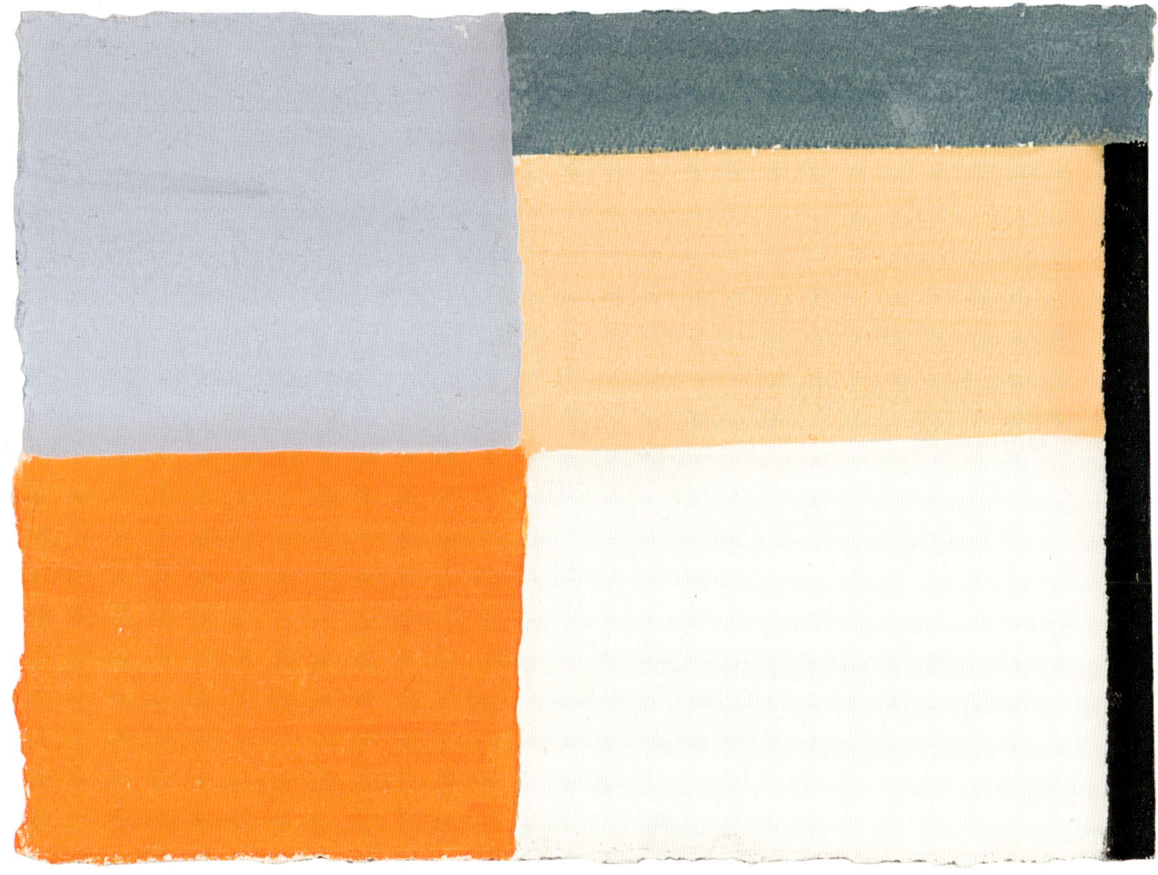

Siteplan Sadiq's House, 2017
Acrylics | Pigment | Handmade paper
9.8 x 13.4 in. | 25 x 34 cm

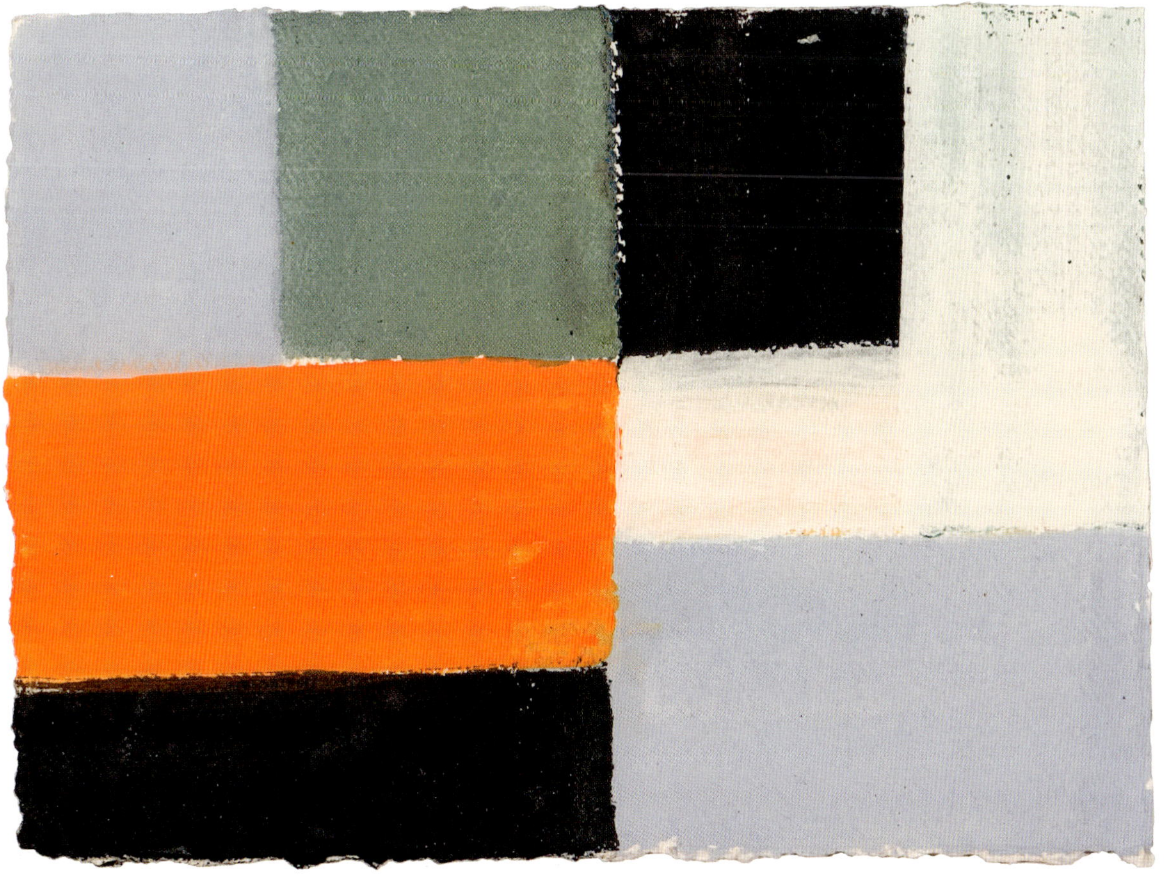

Siteplan Sadiq's House, 2017
Acrylics | Pigment | Handmade paper
9.8 x 13.4 in. | 25 x 34 cm

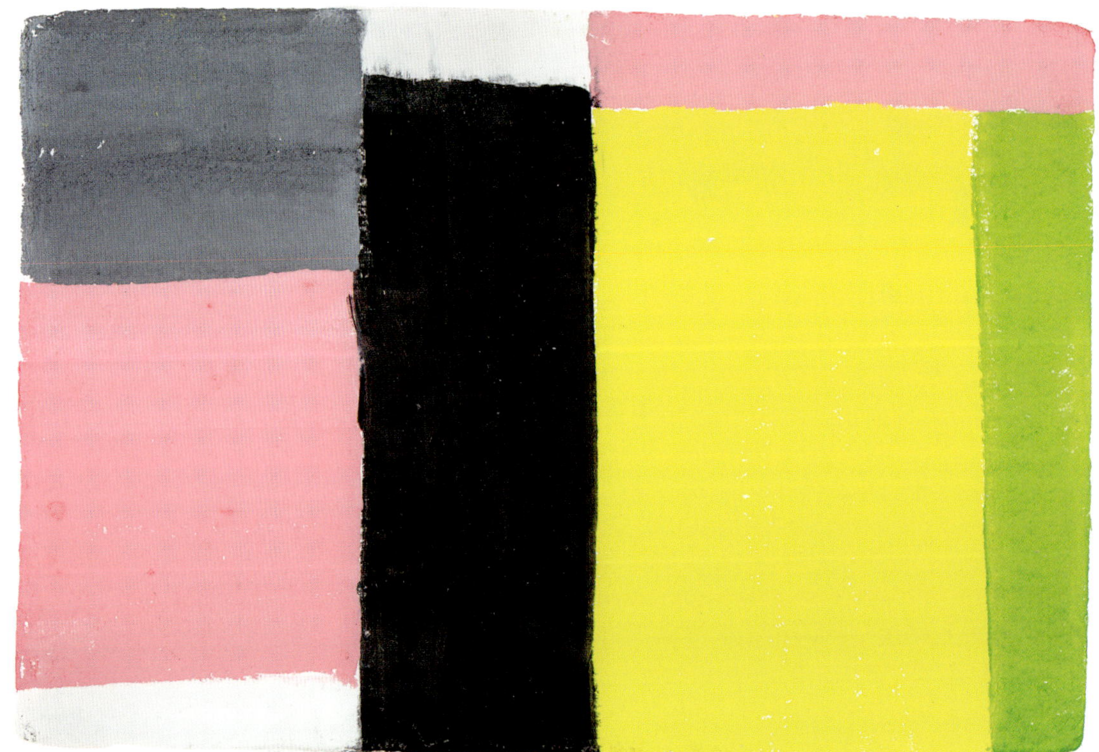

Virginian Siteplan, 2015
Egg tempera | Pigment | Handmade paper
26.8 x 39.4 in. | 68 x 100 cm

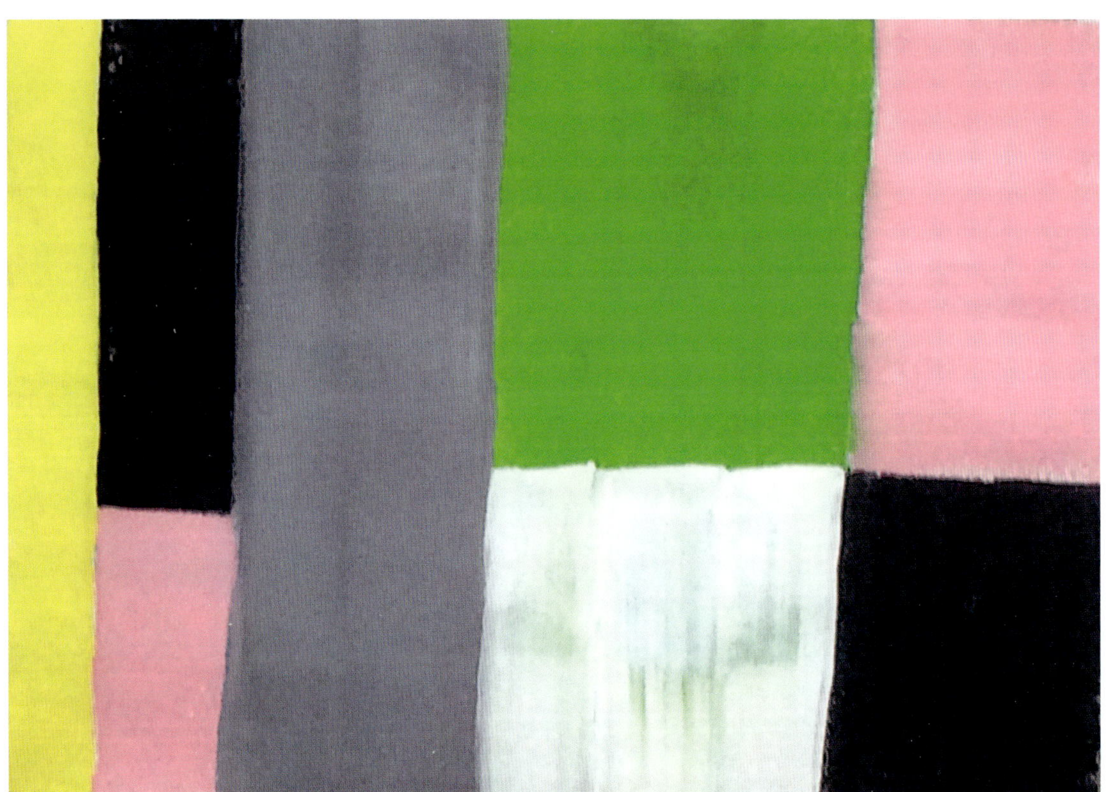

Virginian Siteplan, 2016
Egg tempera | Pigment | Handmade paper
26.8 x 39.4 in. | 68 x 100 cm

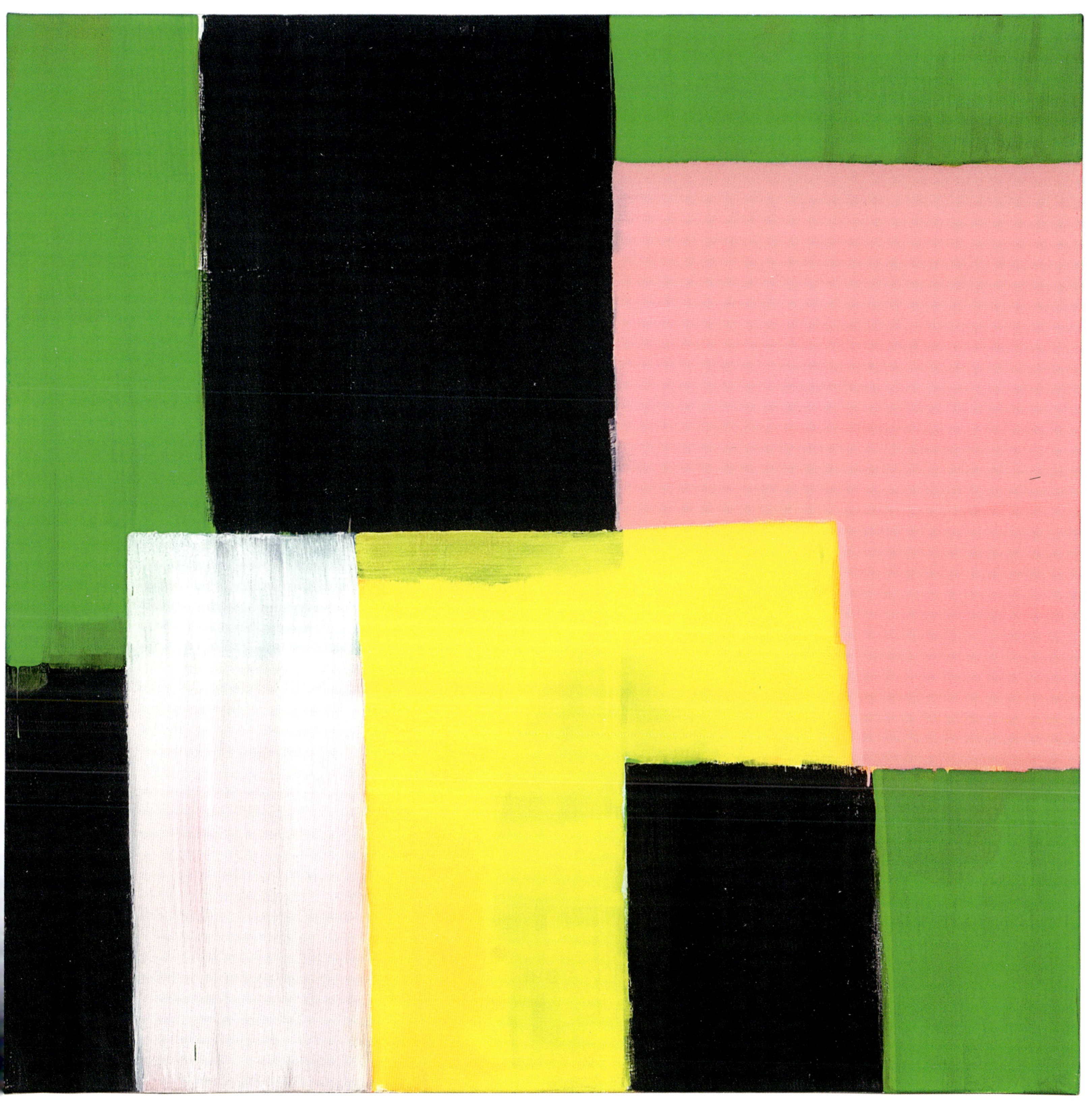

Virginian Siteplan, 2016
Acrylics | Pigment | Canvas
59 x 59 in. | 150 x 150 cm

Virginian Siteplan, 2016
Egg tempera | Pigment | Handmade paper
38.1 x 53.1 in. | 97 x 135 cm

Virginian Siteplan, 2015
Egg tempera | Pigment | Handmade paper
23.6 x 11 in. | 60 x 28 cm

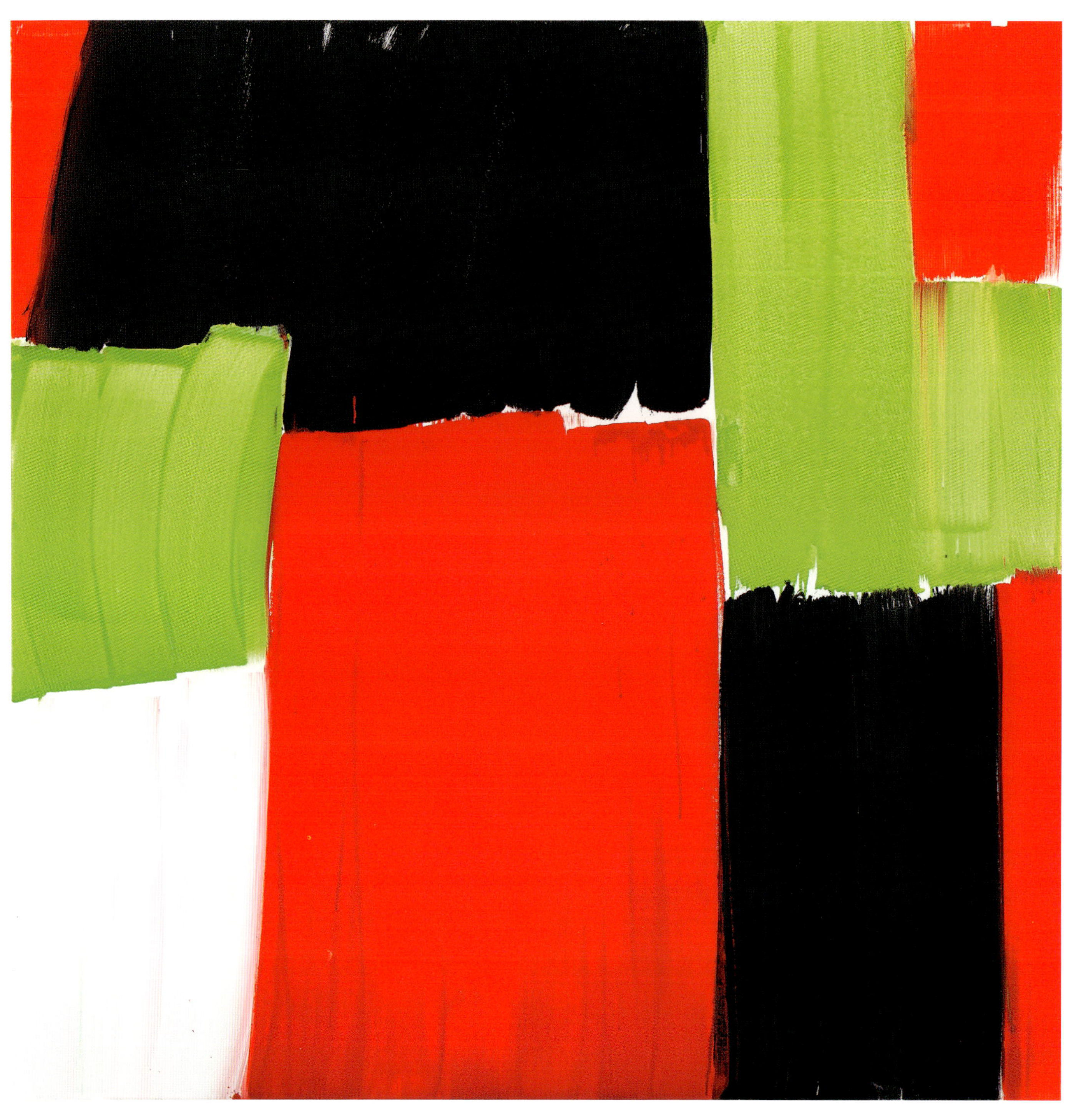

Siteplan Bulgaria, 2014
Egg tempera | Pigment | Canvas
39.4 x 39.4 in. | 100 x 100 cm

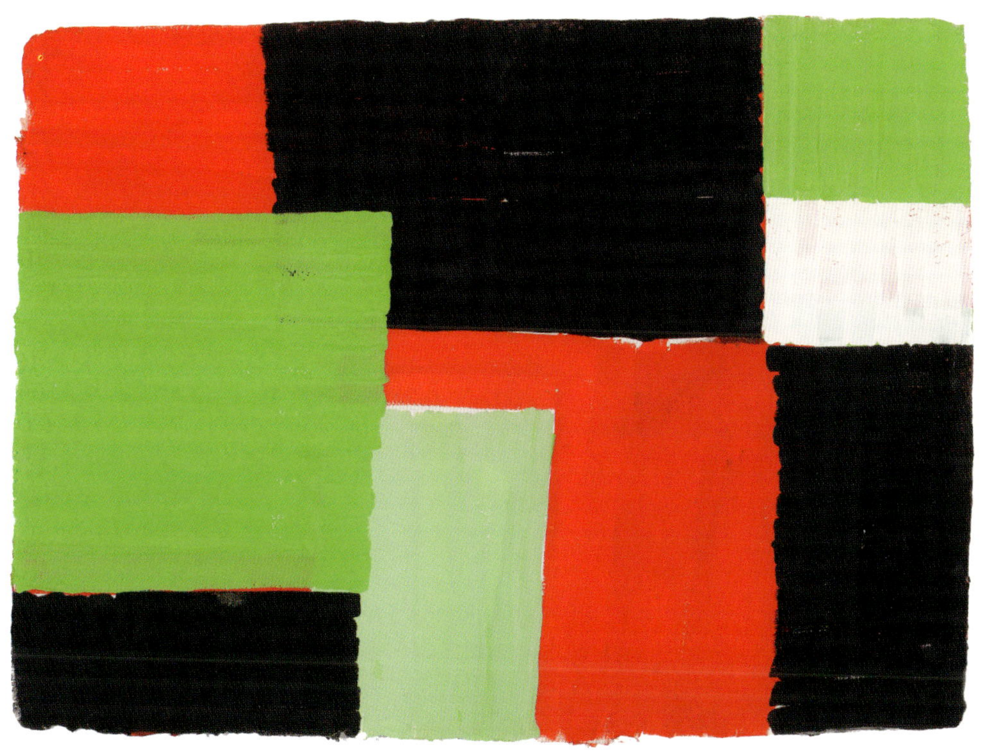

Siteplan Bulgaria, 2014
Egg tempera | Pigment | Handmade Paper
22.8 x 29.2 in. | 58 x 76 cm

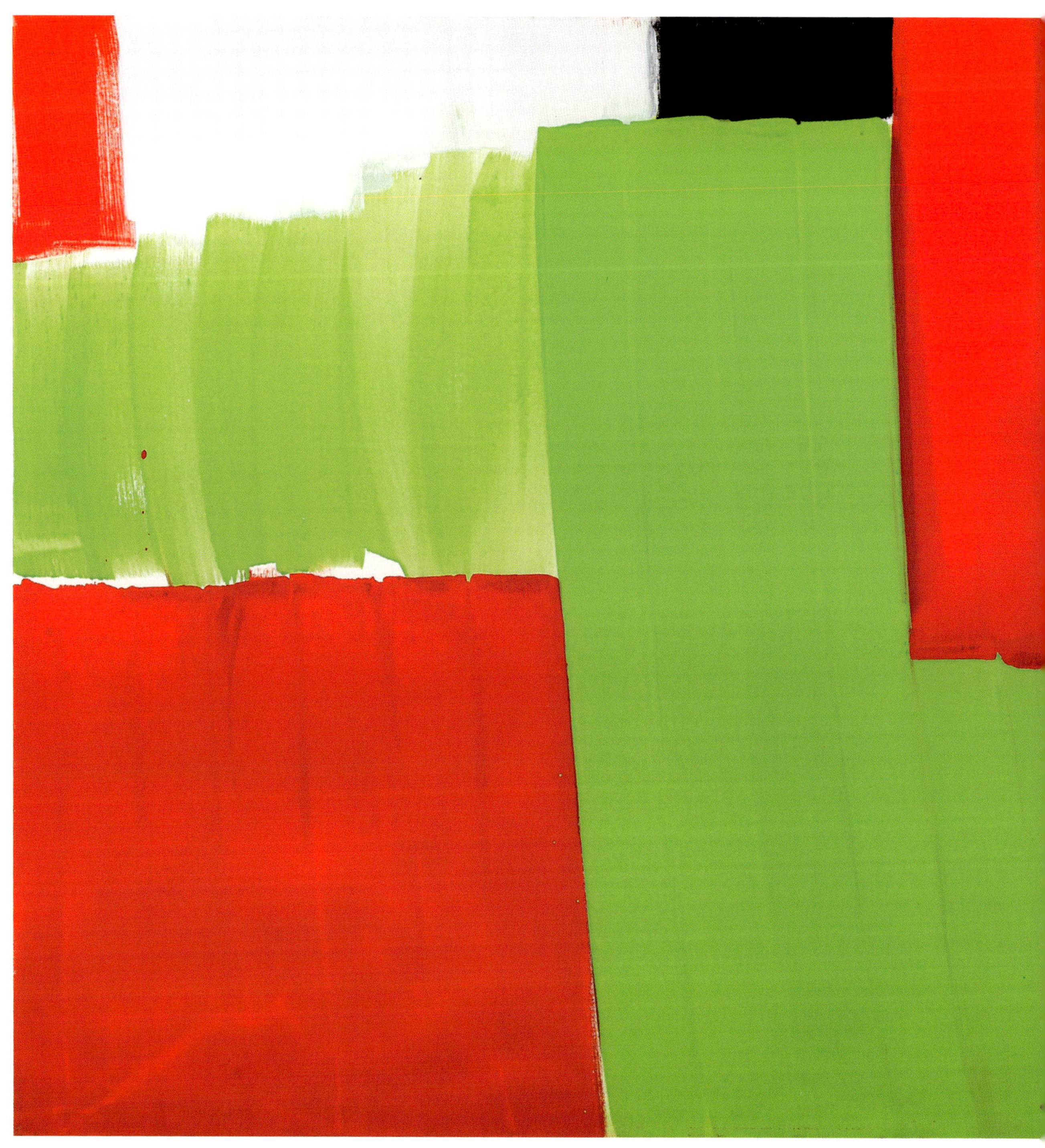

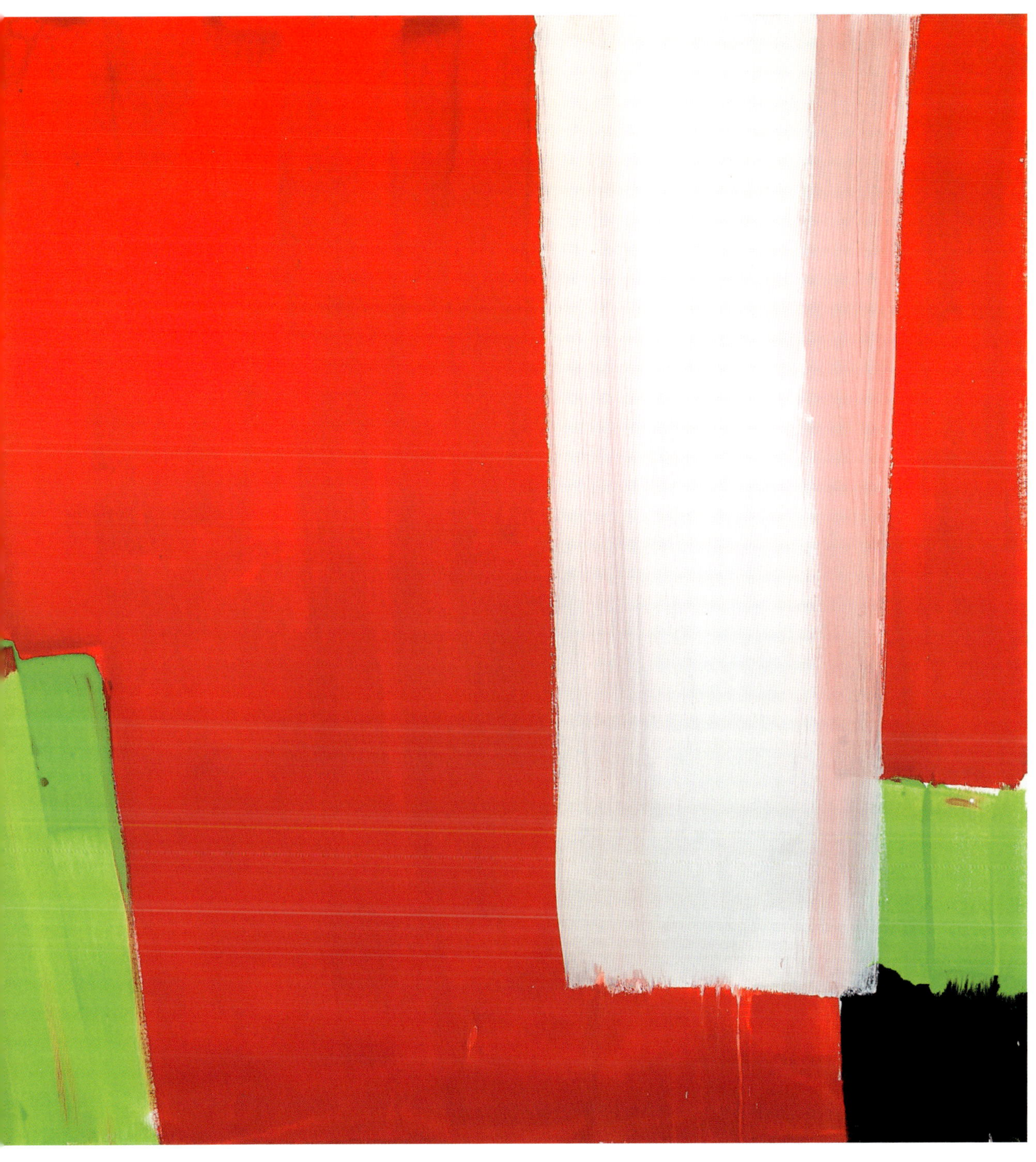

Siteplan Bulgaria, 2014
Diptych
Egg tempera ] Pigment | Canvas
39.4 x 78.7 in. | 100 x 200 cm

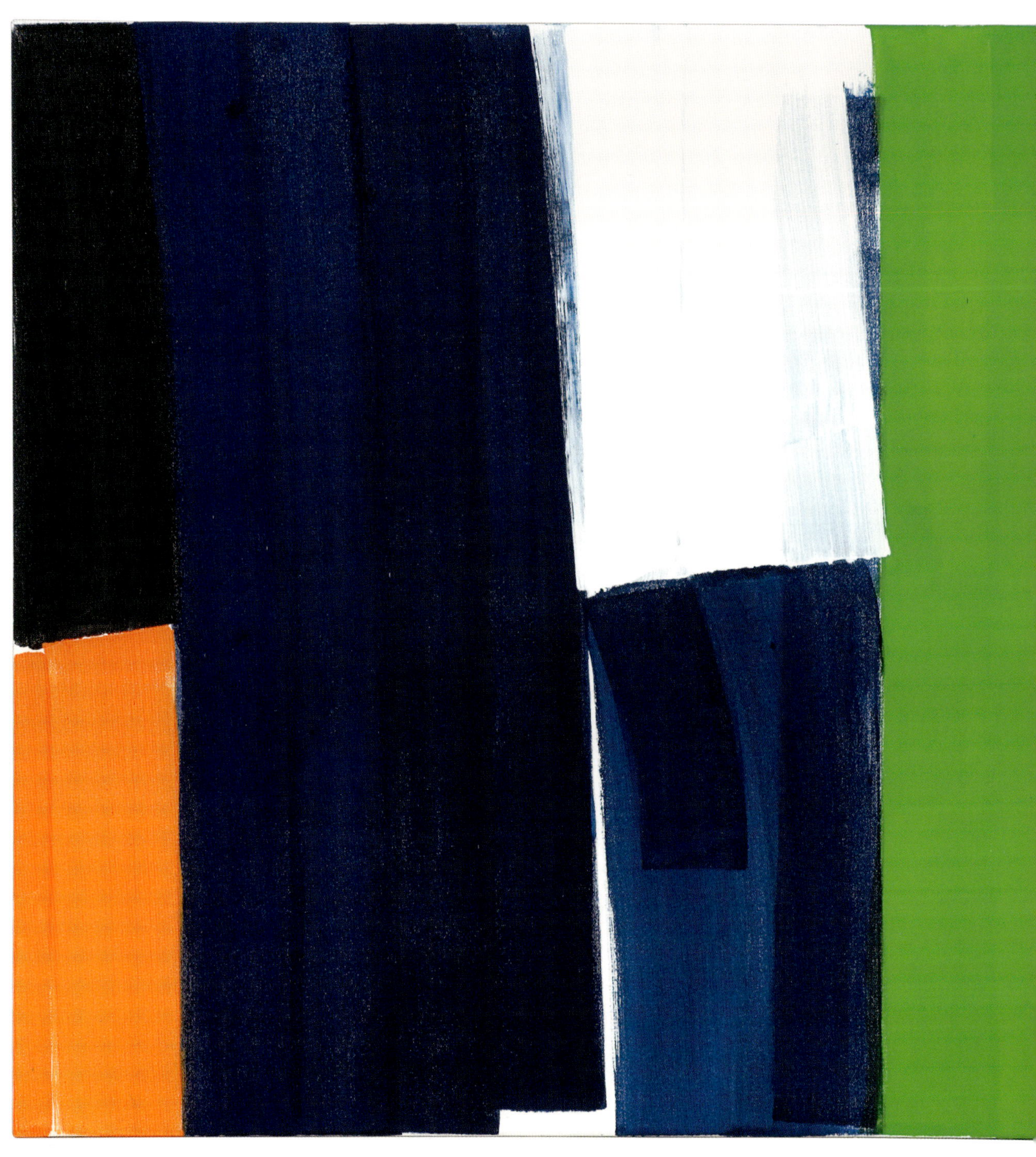

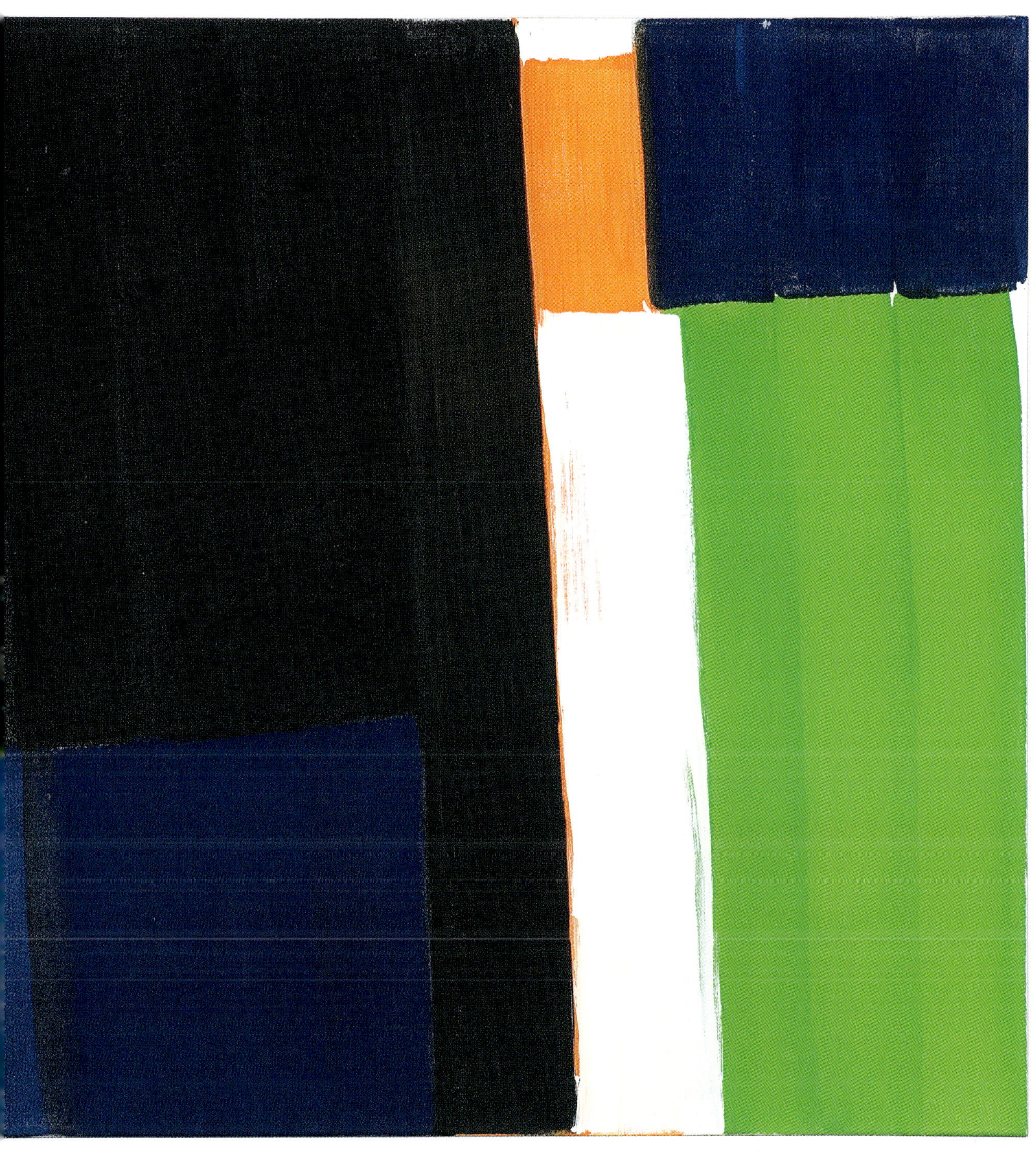

Siteplan Blue, Green, Orange, 2015
Diptych
Acrylics | Pigment | Canvas
39.4 x 78.7 in. | 100 x 200 cm

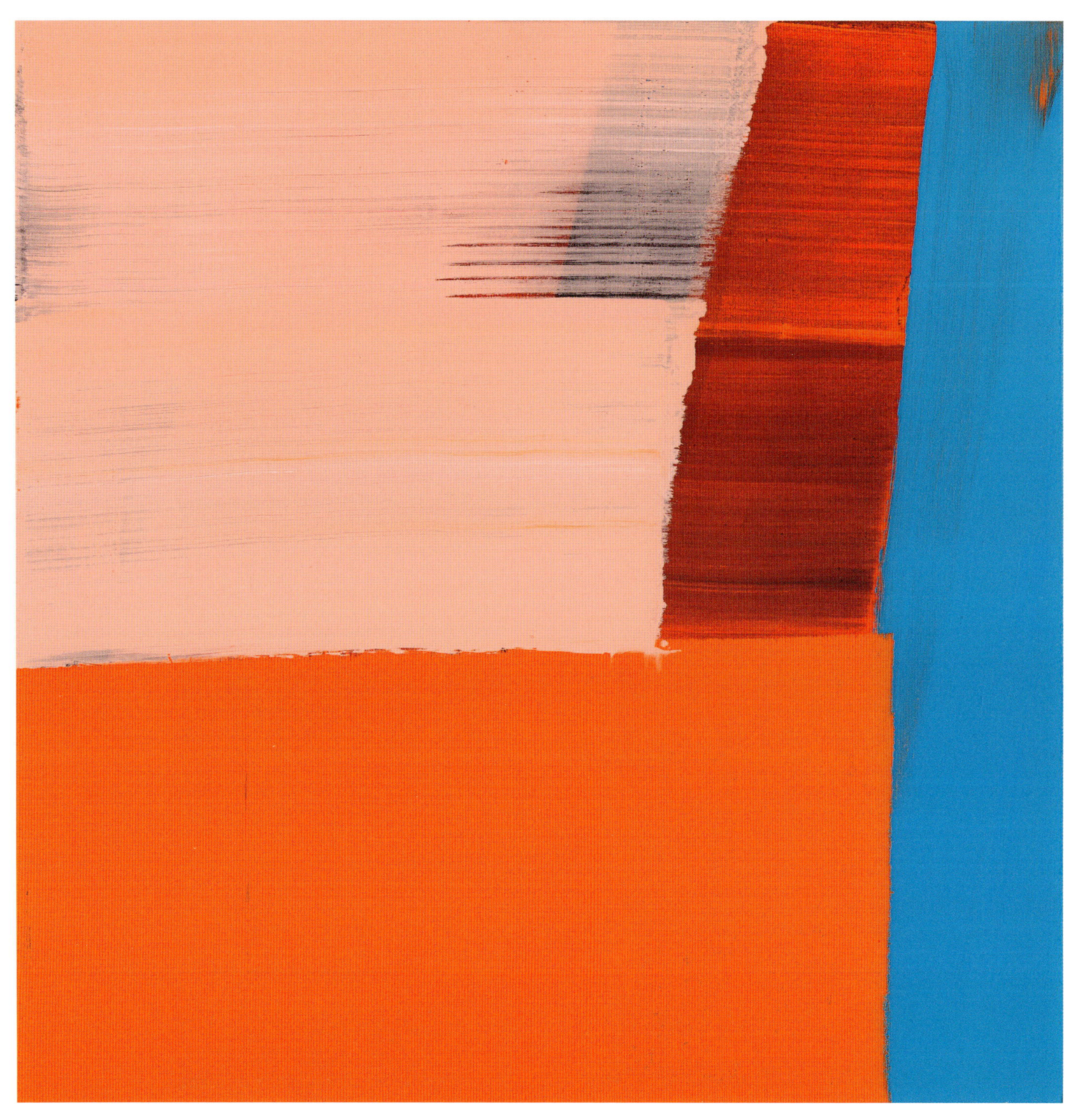

Siteplan Orange, Blue, 2013
Acrylics | Pigment | Canvas
39.4 x 39.4 in. | 100 x 100 cm

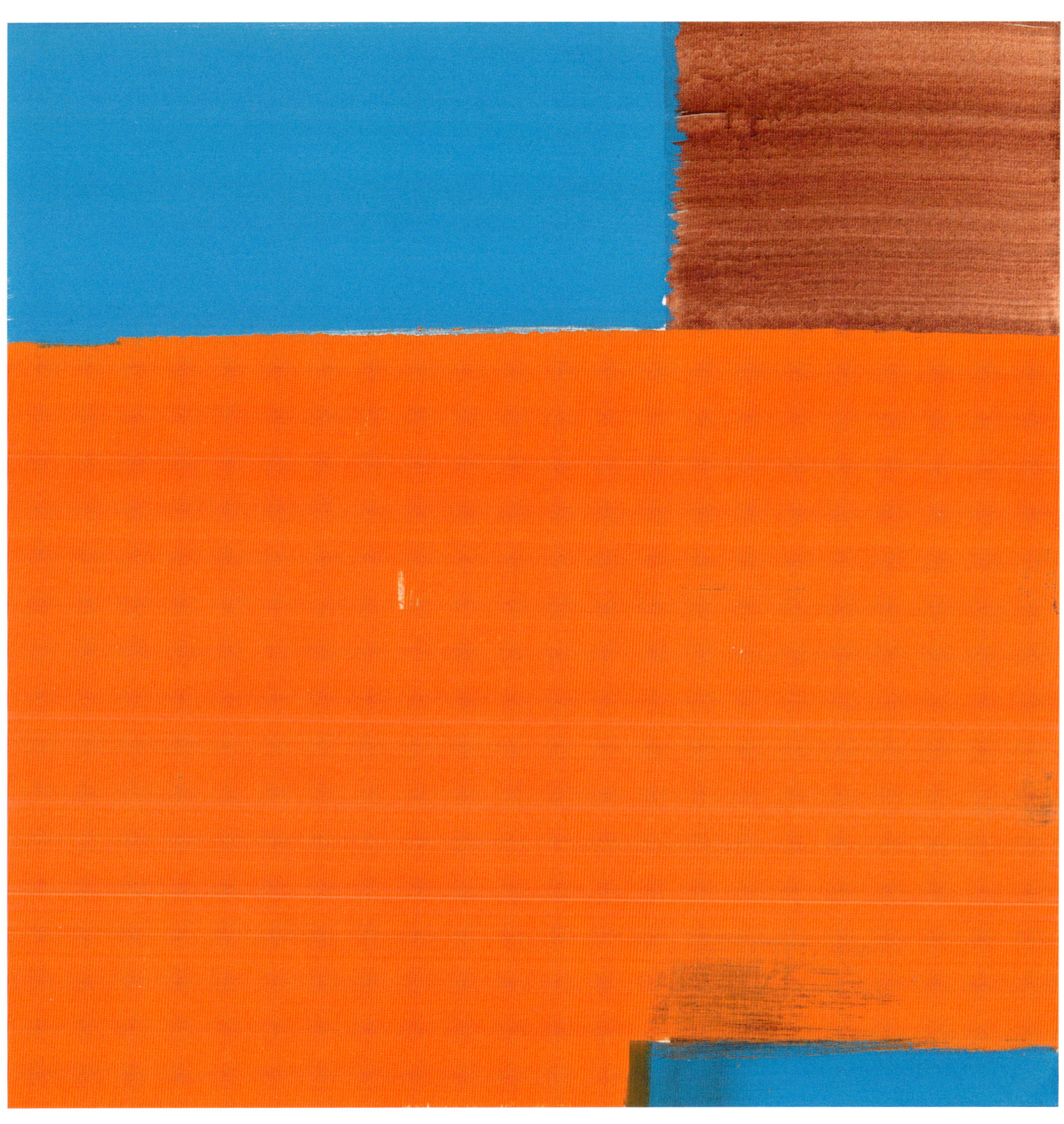

Siteplan Orange, Blue, 2013
Acrylics | Pigment | Canvas
39.4 x 39.4 in. | 100 x 100 cm

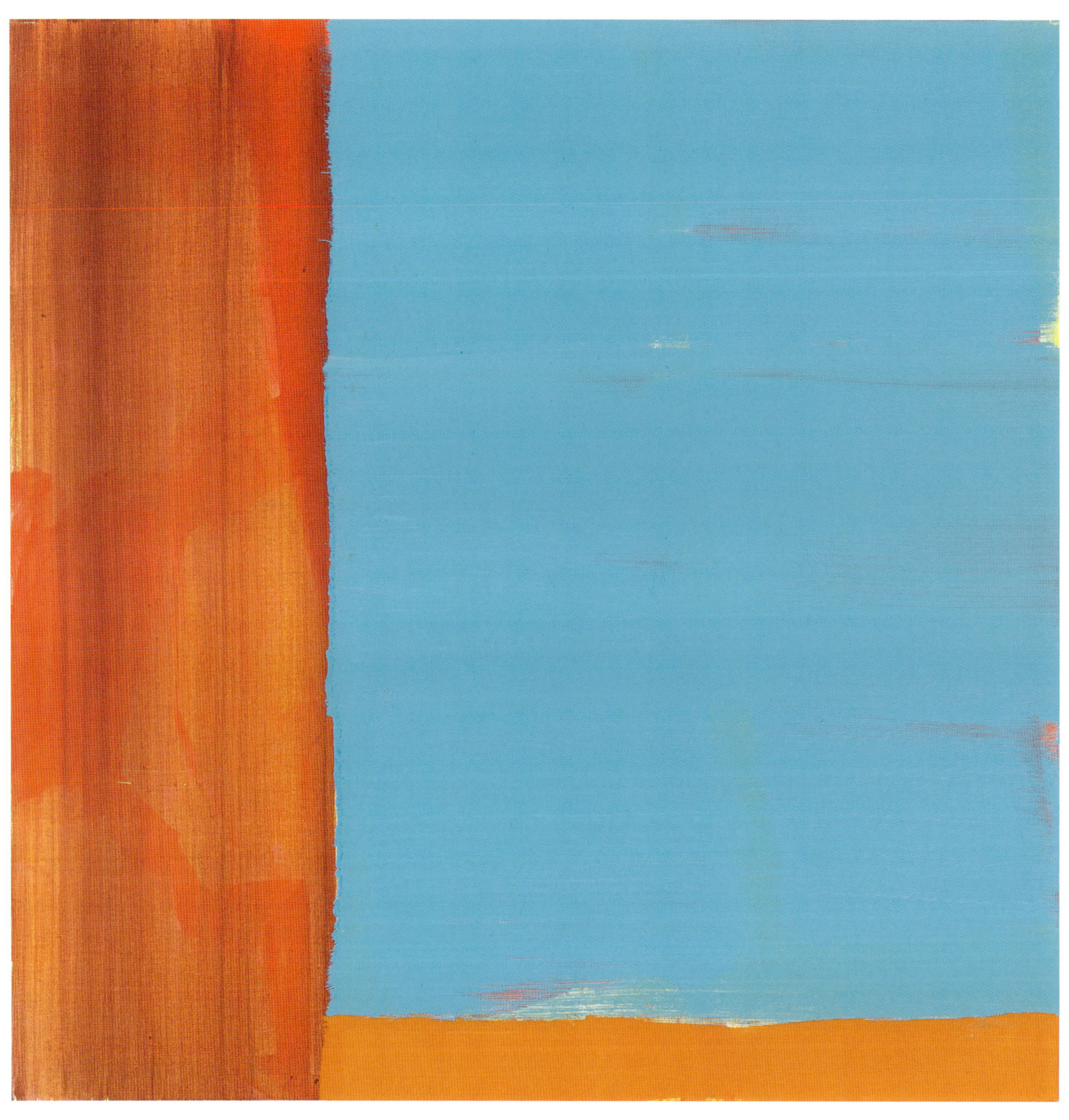

Siteplan Orange, Blue, 2013
Acrylics | Pigment | Canvas
39.4 x 39.4 in. | 100 x 100 cm

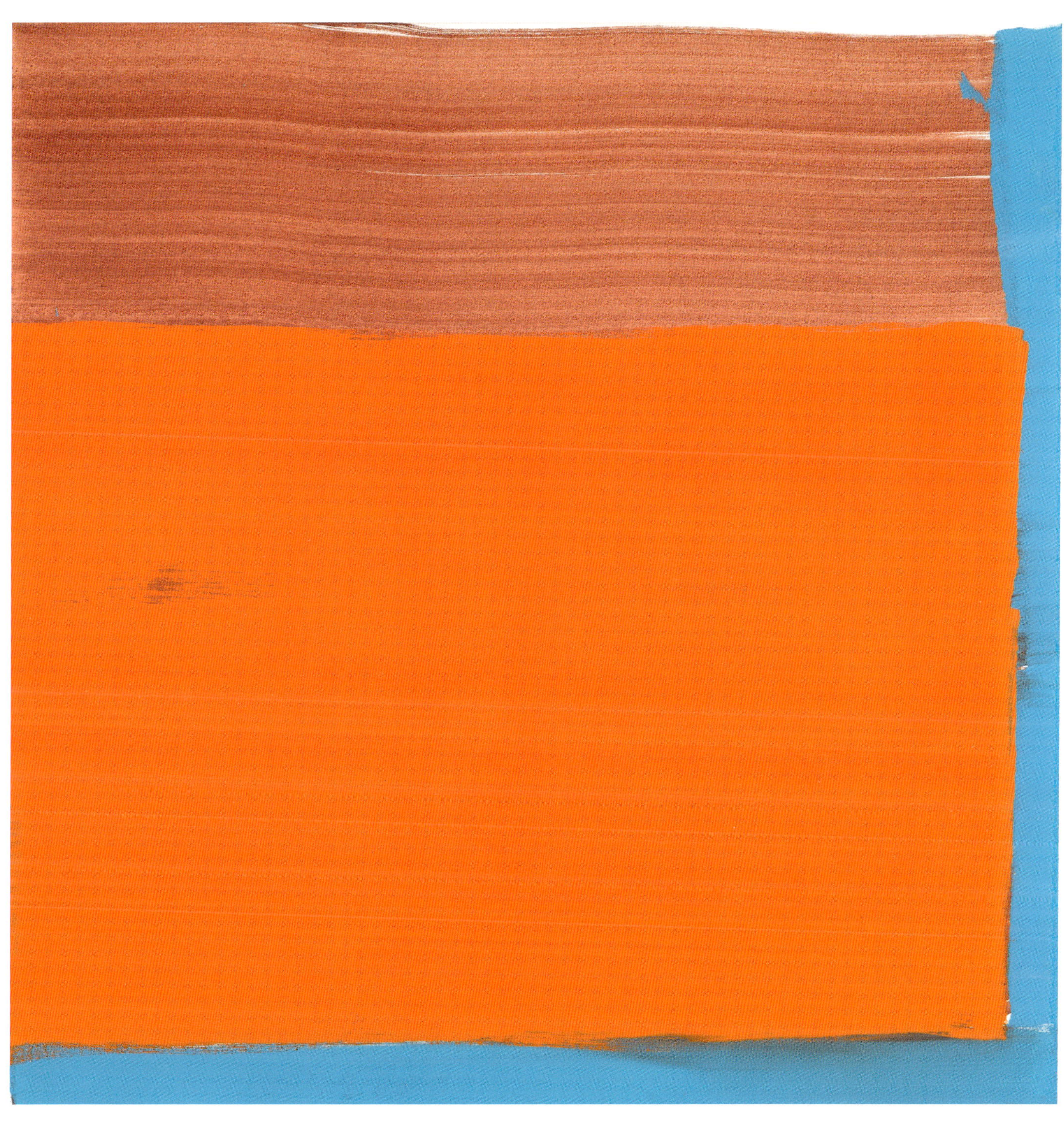

Siteplan Orange, Blue, 2013
Acrylics | Pigment | Canvas
39.4 x 39.4 in. | 100 x 100 cm

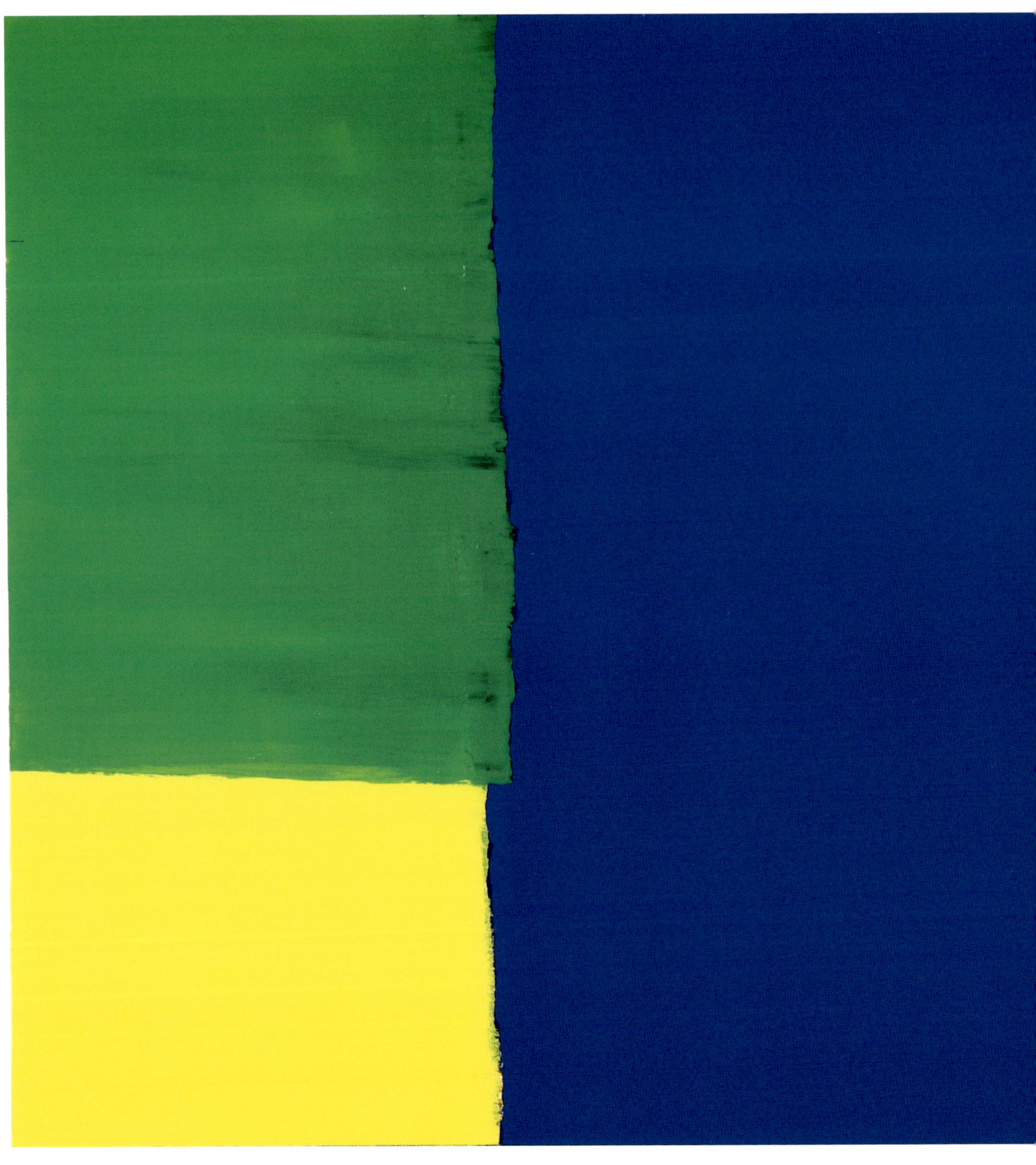

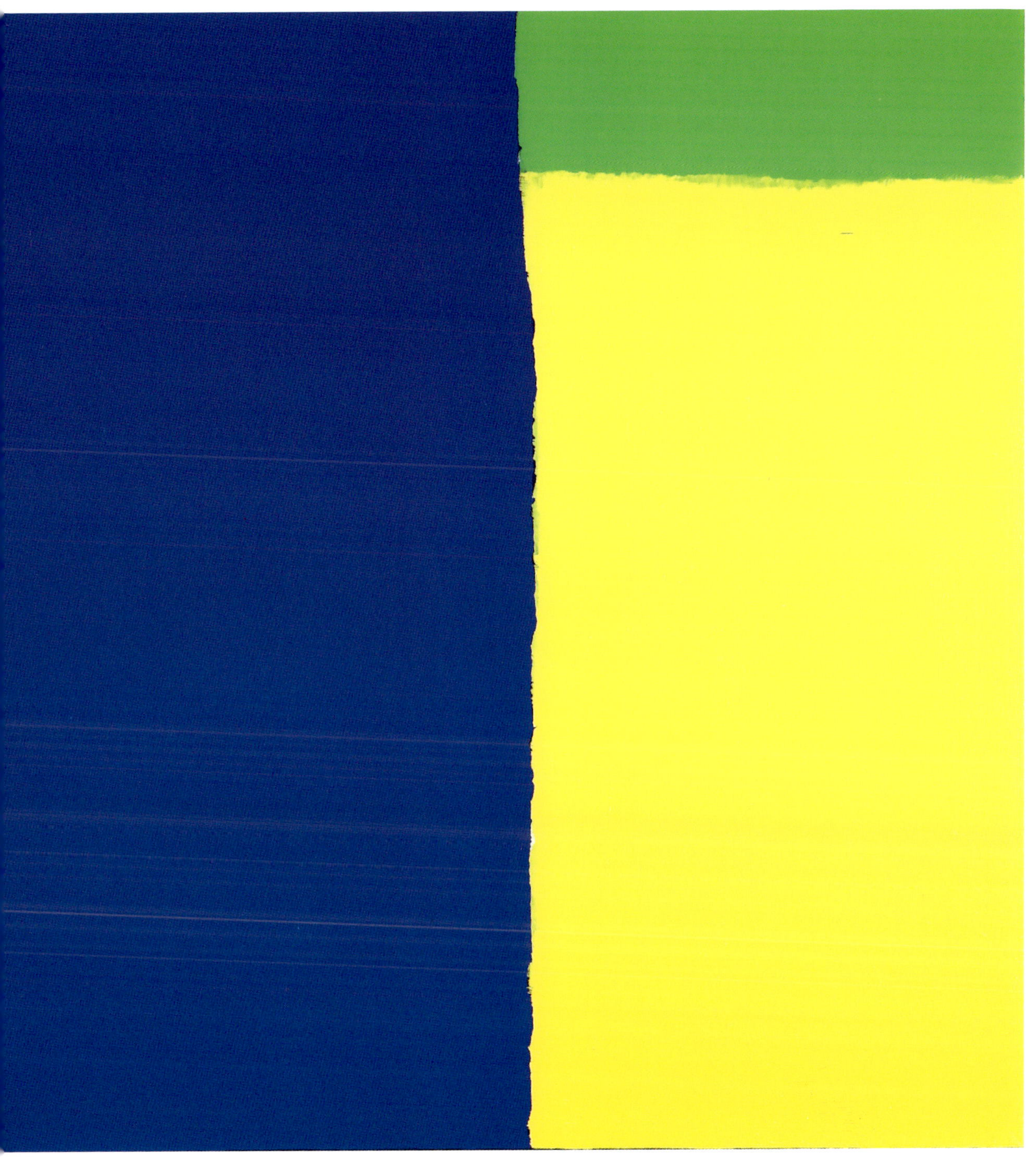

Siteplan Blue, Yellow, Green, 2009
Diptych
Acrylics | Pigment | Canvas
39.4 x 78.7 in. | 100 x 200 cm
Private collection

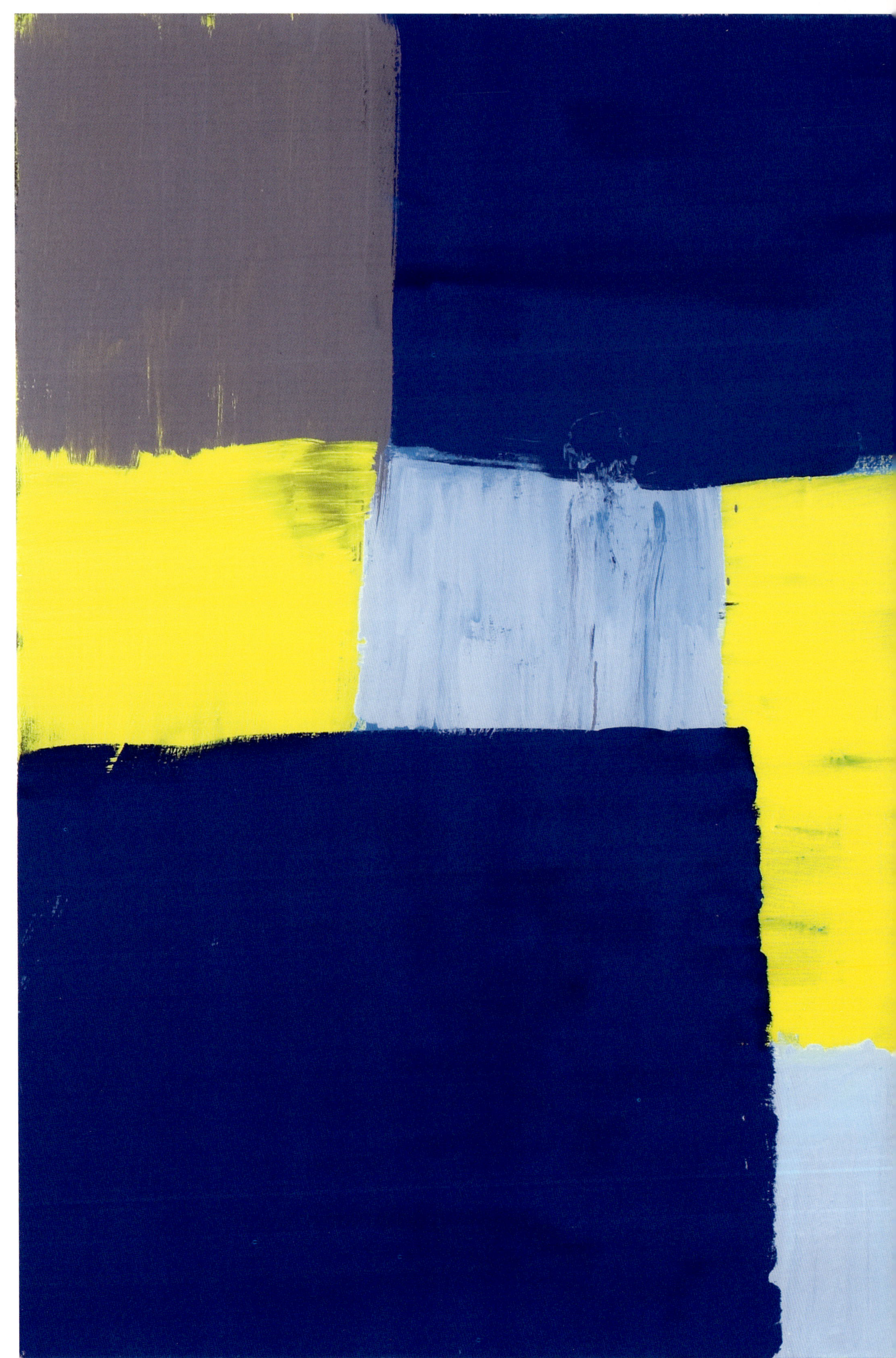

Siteplan Dark-blue, Yellow, 2009
Acrylics | Pigment | Canvas
55.1 x 78.7 in. | 140 x 200 cm

Siteplan San Angelo Drive, 2015
Egg tempera | Pigment | Handmade paper
9.8 x 13.4 in. | 25 x 34 cm

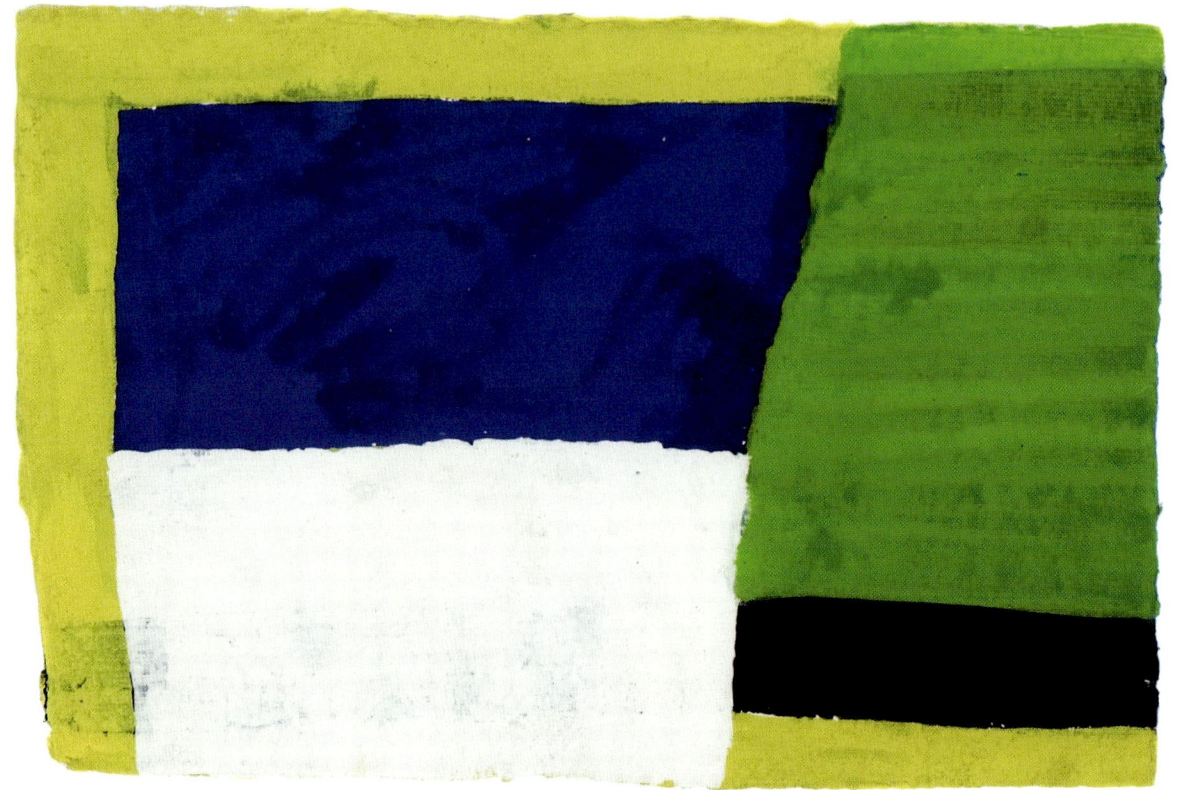

Siteplan San Angelo Drive, 2015
Egg tempera | Pigment | Handmade paper
9.8 x 13.4 in. | 25 x 34 cm

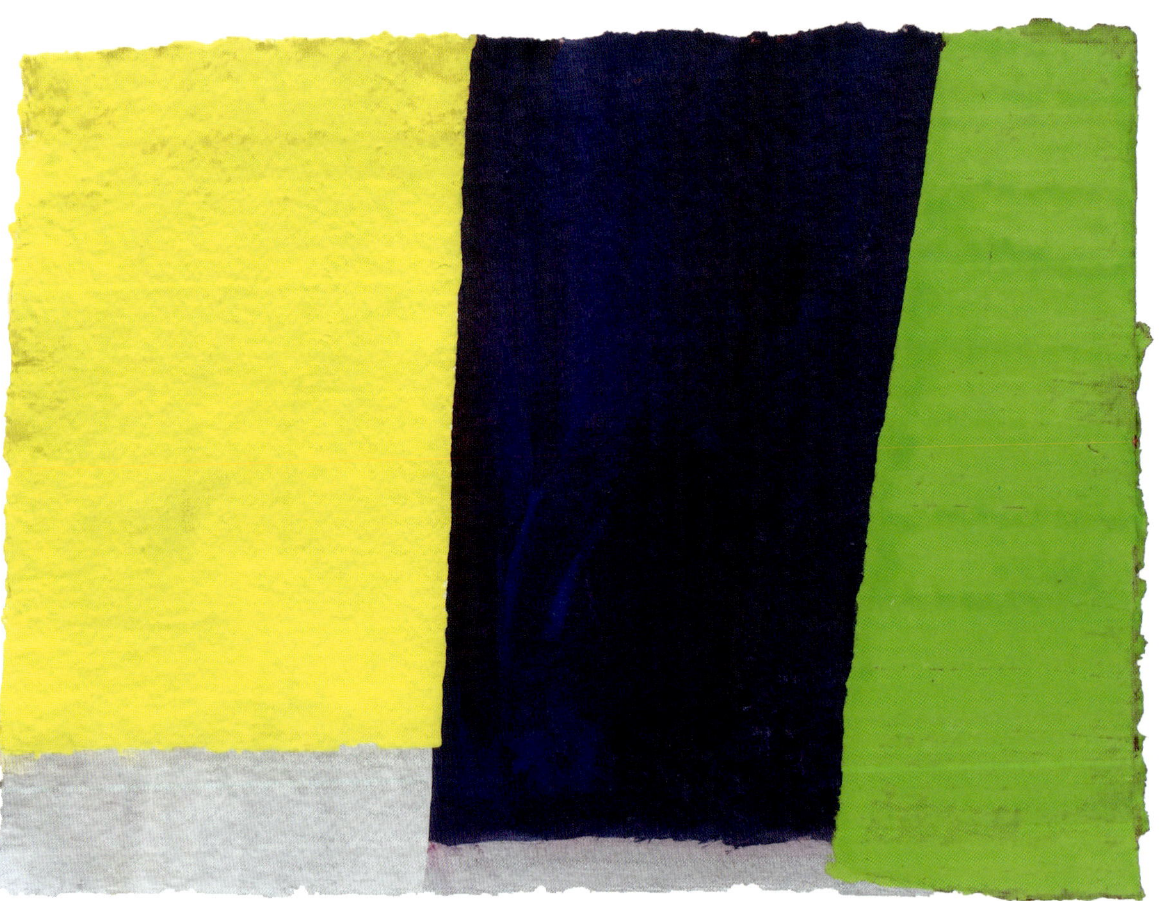

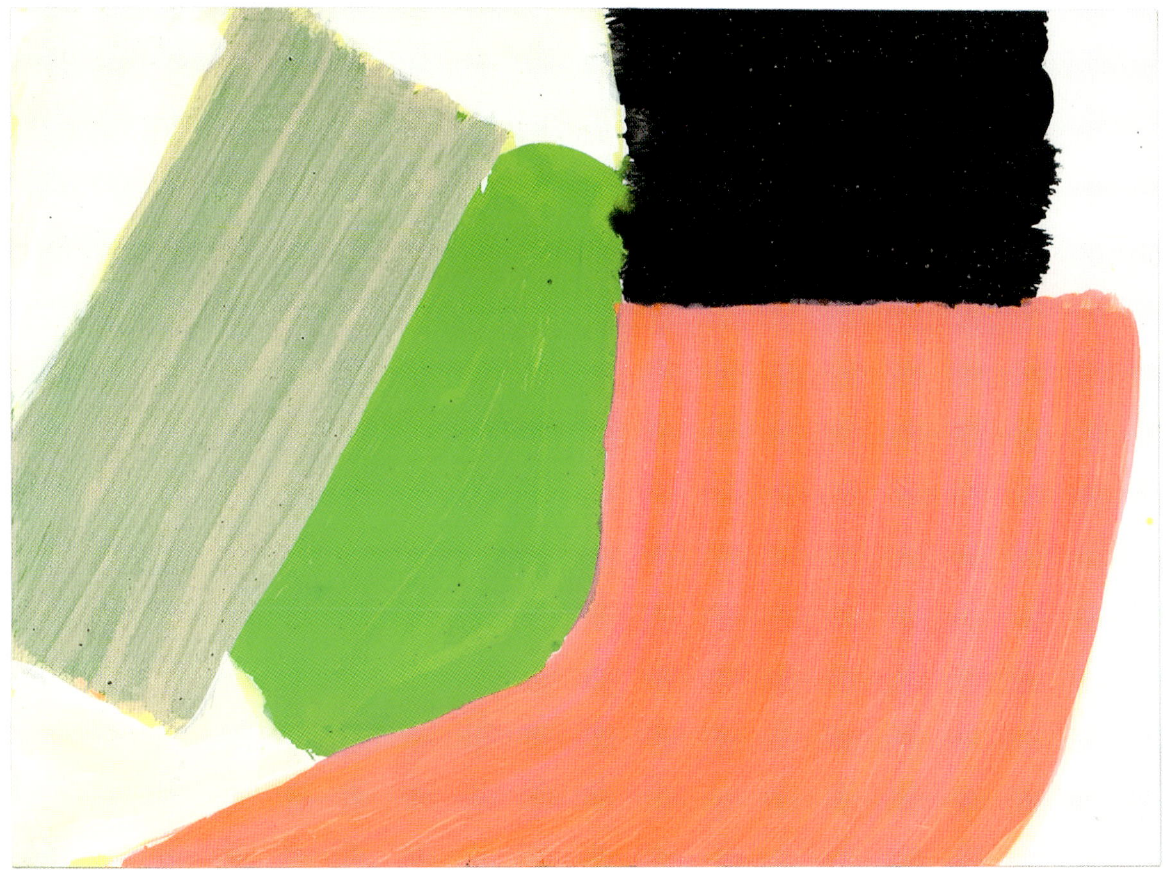

Siteplan Barn Complex, 2015
Egg tempera | Pigment | Cardboard
9 x 11.8 in. | 23 x 30 cm

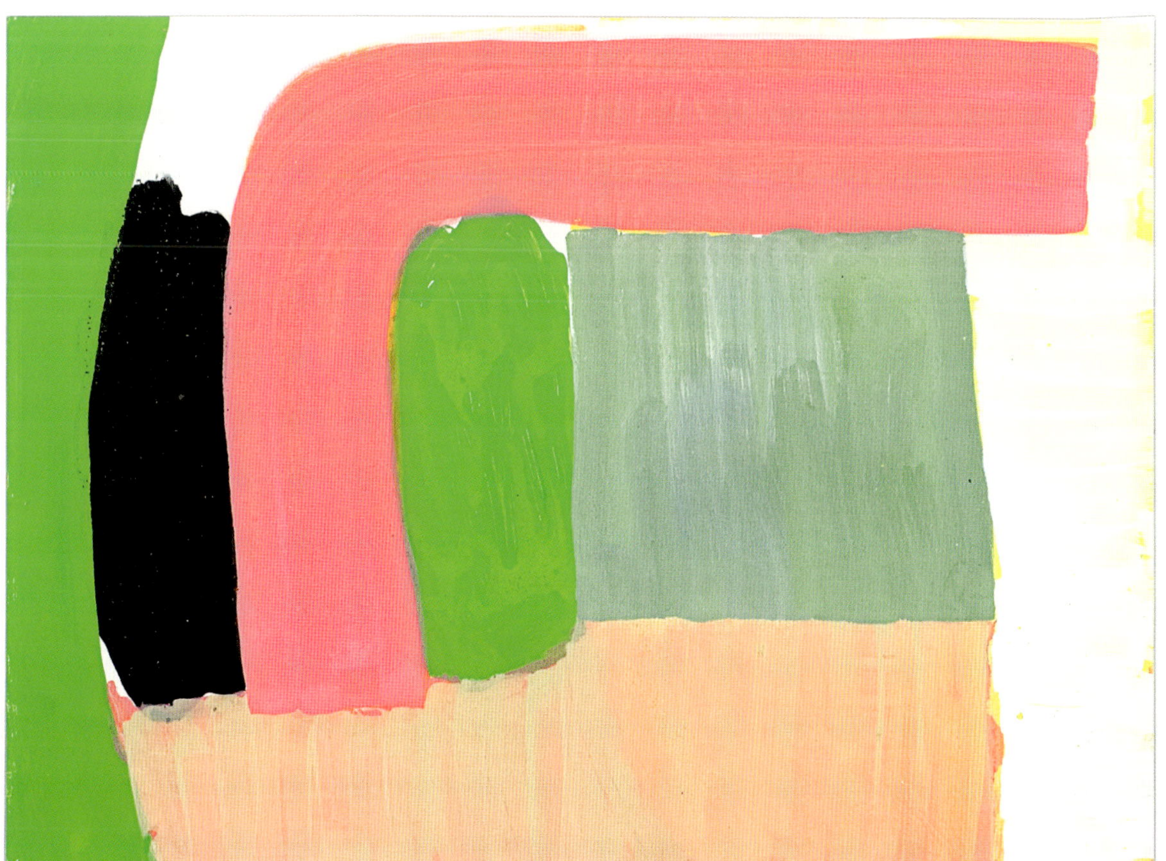

Siteplan Barn Complex, 2015
Egg tempera | Pigment | Cardboard
9 x 11.8 in. | 23 x 30 cm

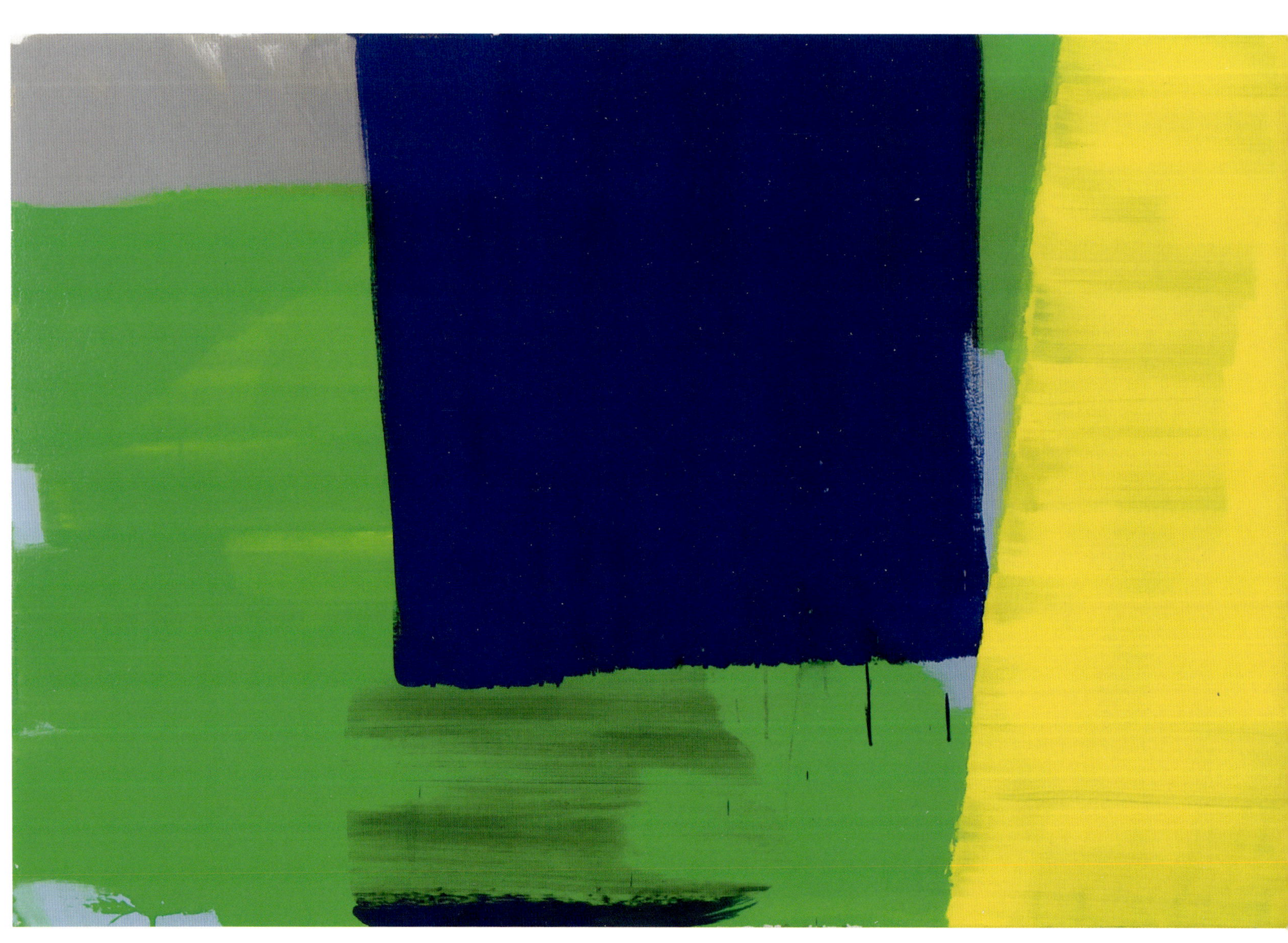

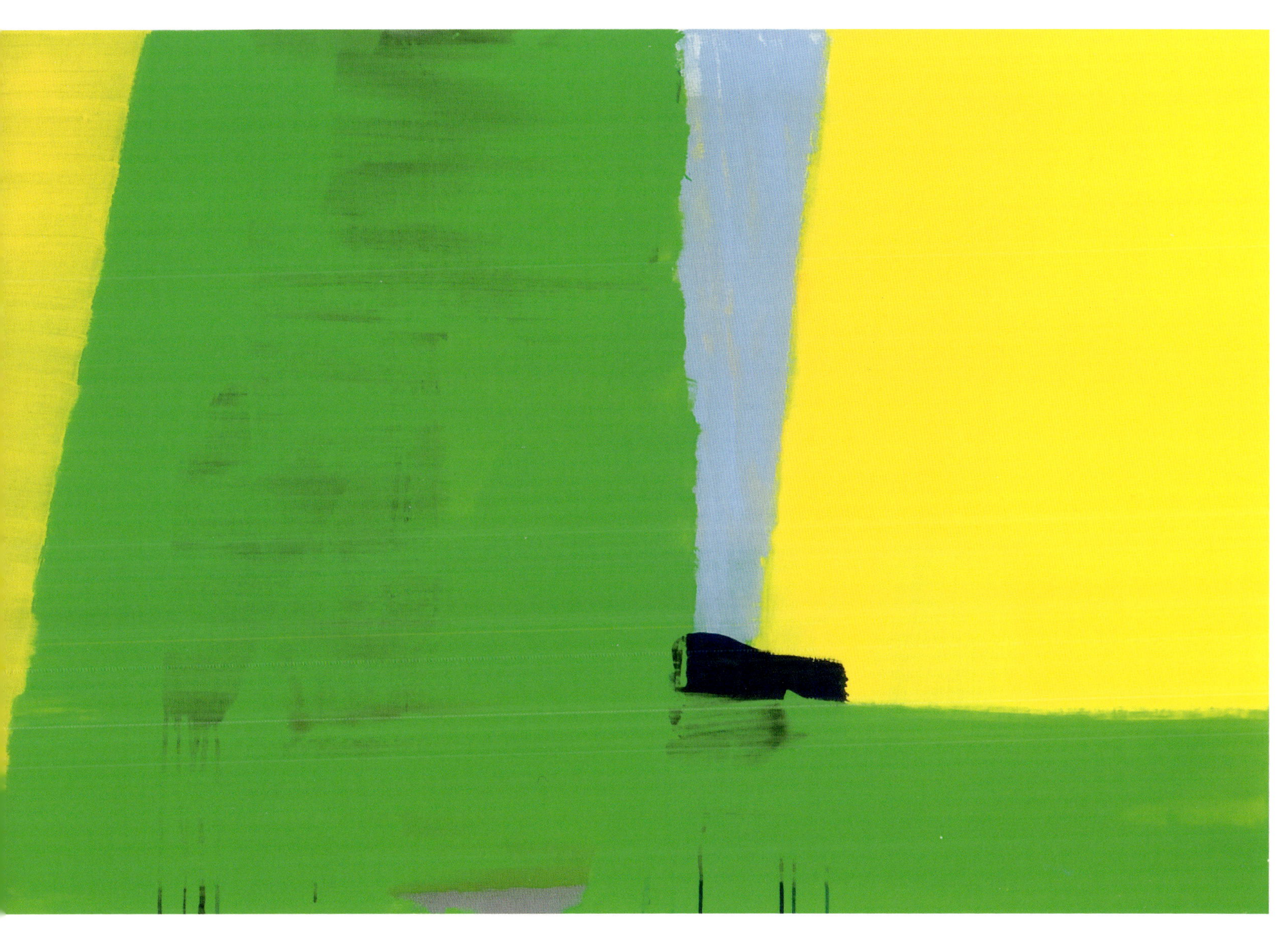

Siteplan Blue, Green, Yellow, 2009
Diptych
Acrylics | Pigment | Canvas
35.4 x 110.2 in. | 90 x 280 cm
Public collection

Siteplan Lock, 2013
Egg tempera | Pigment | Canvas
19.7 x 19.7 in. | 50 x 50 cm

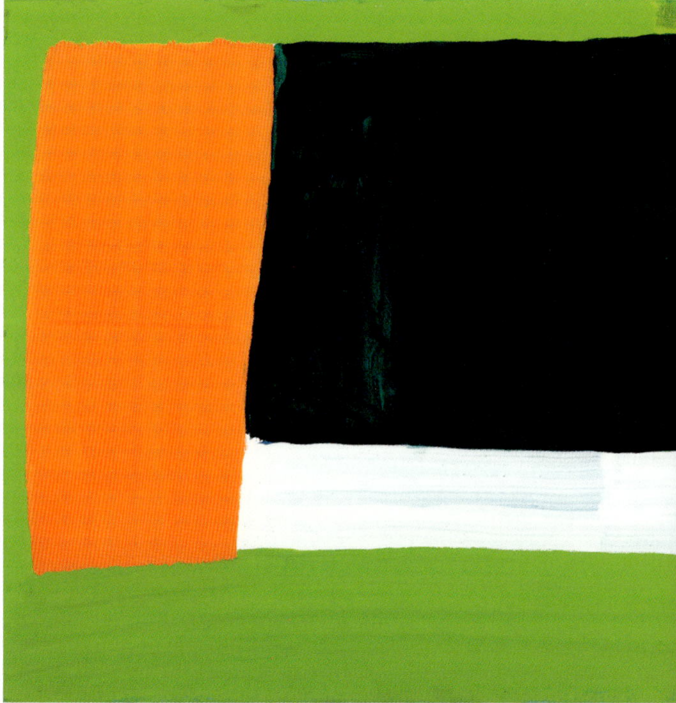

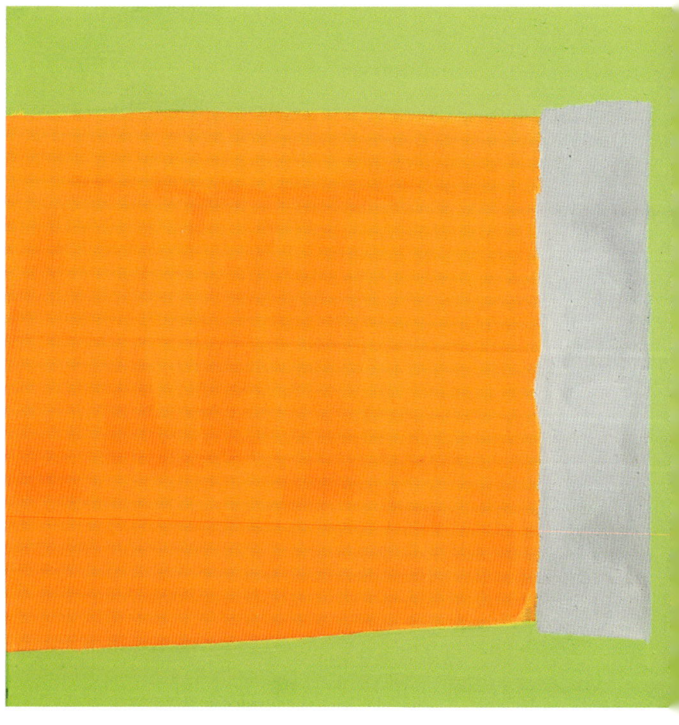

ABOVE:
Siteplan Bremerhaven, 2013
Egg tempera | Pigment | Canvas
19.7 x 19.7 in. | 50 x 50 cm

BELOW:
Siteplan Harbour, 2013
Egg tempera | Pigment | Canvas
19.7 x 19.7 in. | 50 x 50 cm

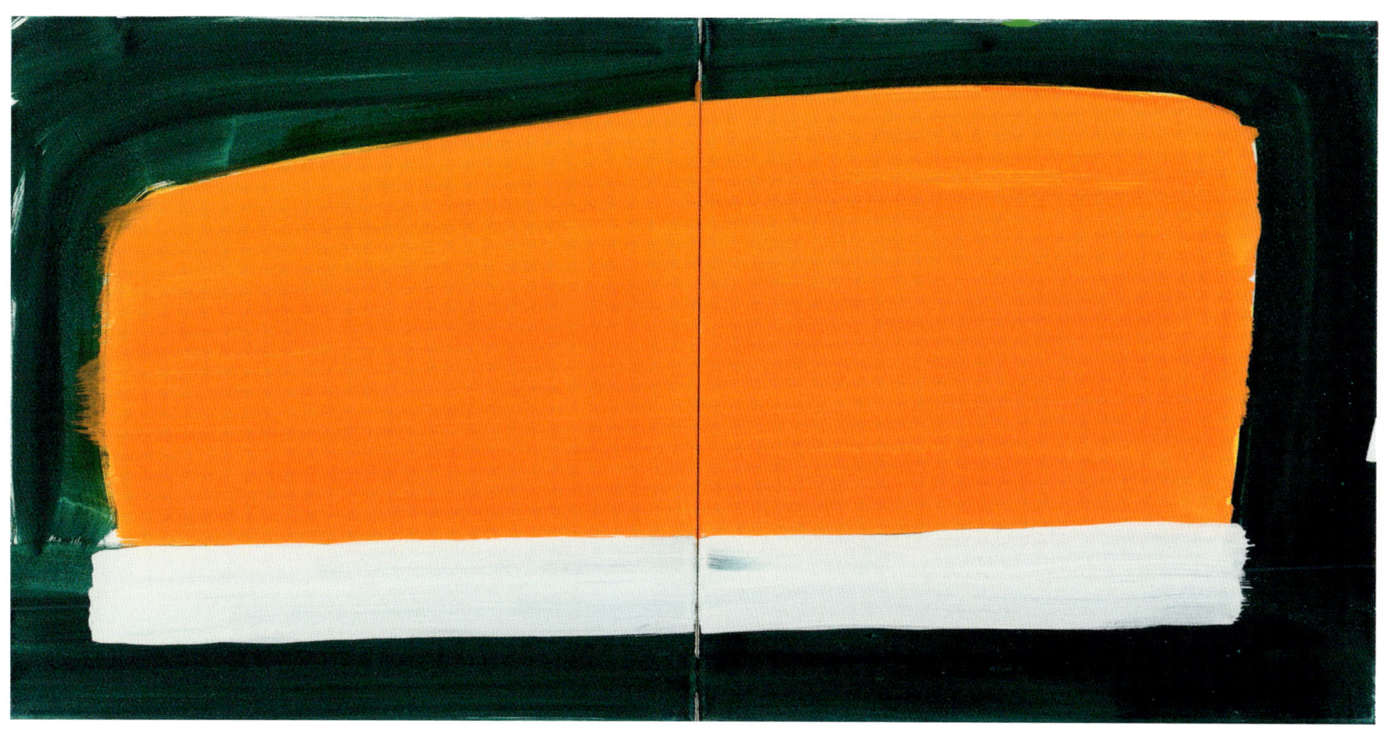

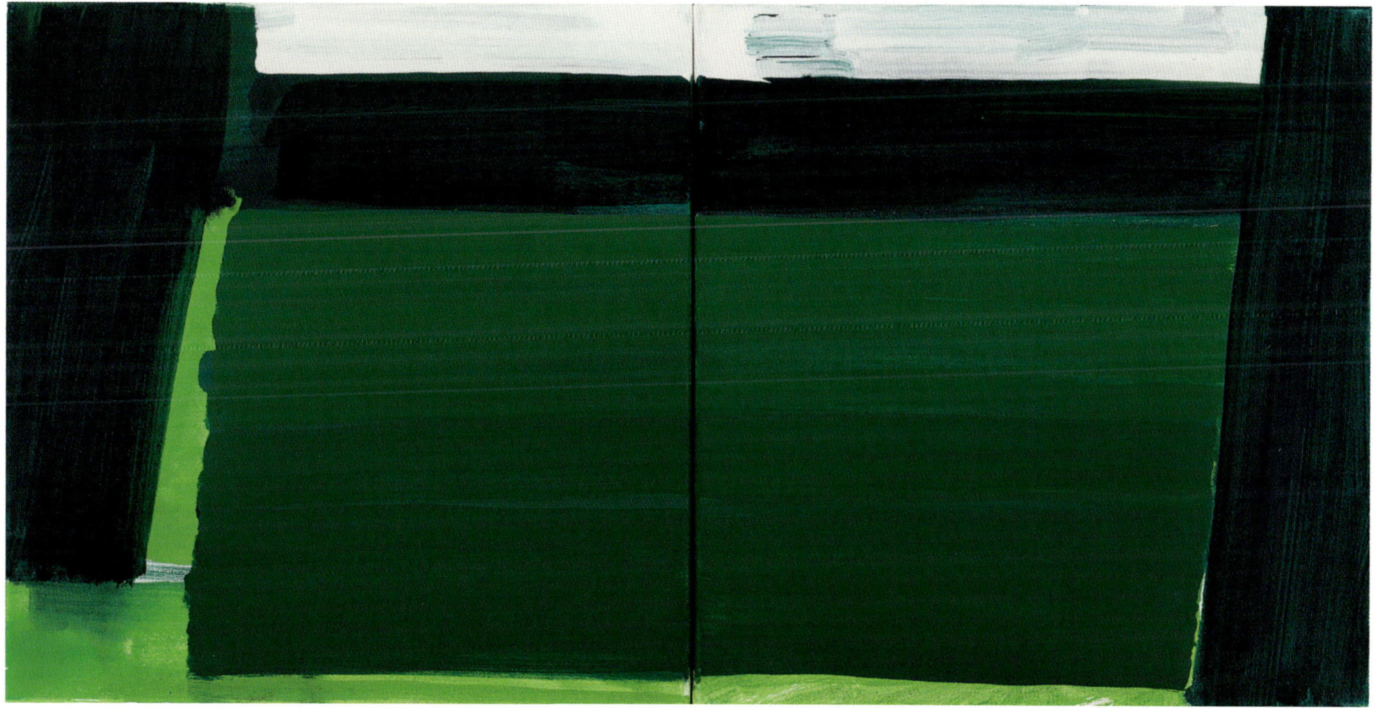

ABOVE:
Siteplan Bremerhaven Germany, 2014
Diptych
Egg tempera | Pigment | Canvas
19.7 x 39.4 in. | 50 x 100 cm

BELOW:
Siteplan Lock, 2013
Diptych
Egg tempera | Pigment | Canvas
19.7 x 39.4 in. | 50 x 100 cm

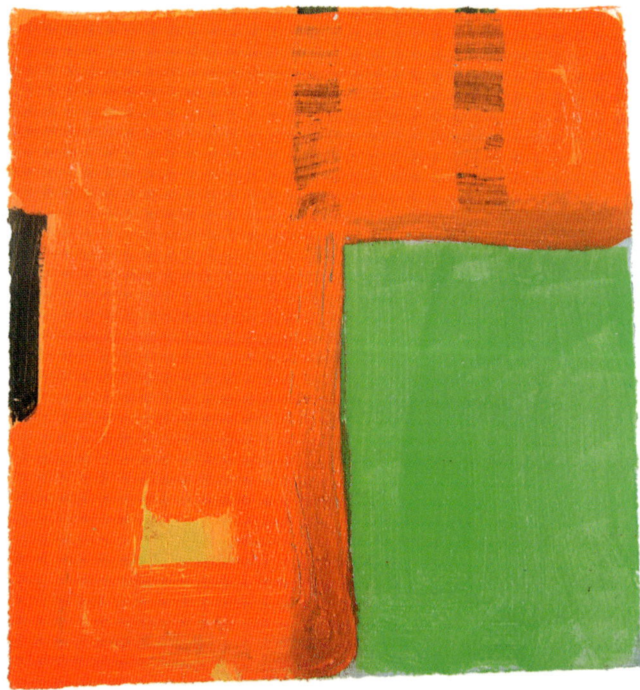

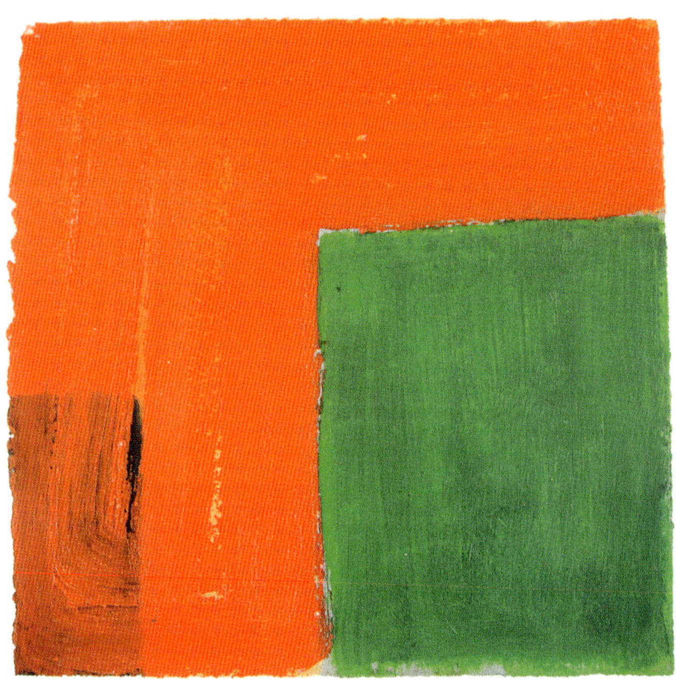

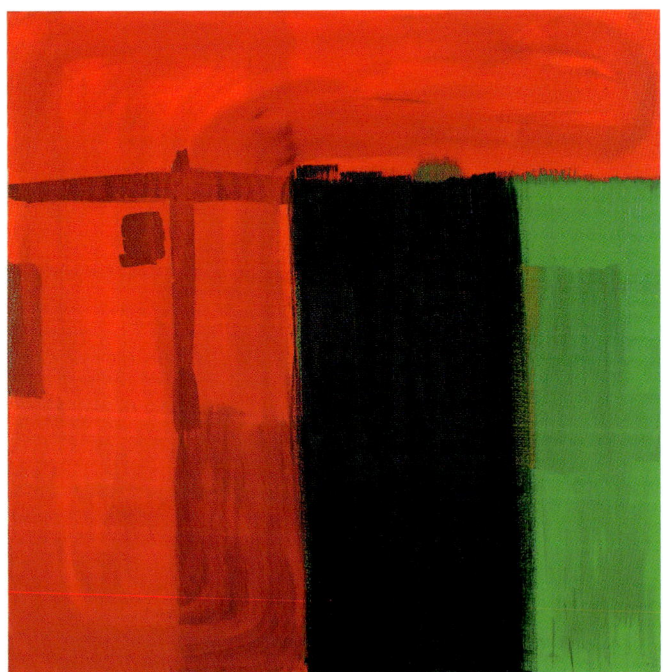

ABOVE:
Siteplan Studio E.B., 2011
Acrylics | Pigment | Handmade paper
7.9 x 7.9 in. | 20 x 20 cm

BELOW:
Siteplan Studio E.B., 2011
Acrylics | Pigment | Handmade paper
7.9 x 7.9 in. | 20 x 20 cm

ABOVE:
Siteplan Studio E.B., 2011
Acrylics | Pigment | Handmade paper
7.9 x 7.9 in. | 20 x 20 cm

BELOW:
Siteplan Studio E.B., 2011
Acrylics | Pigment | Canvas
43.3 x 43.3 in. | 20 x 20 cm

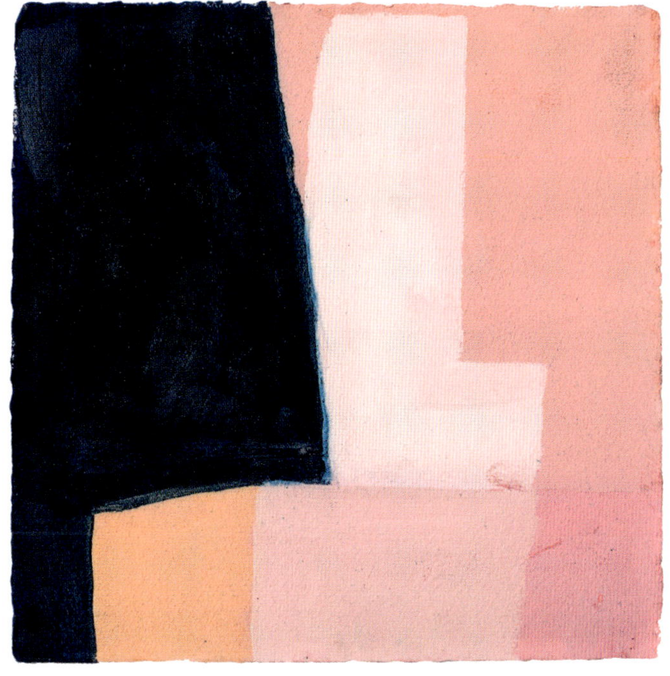

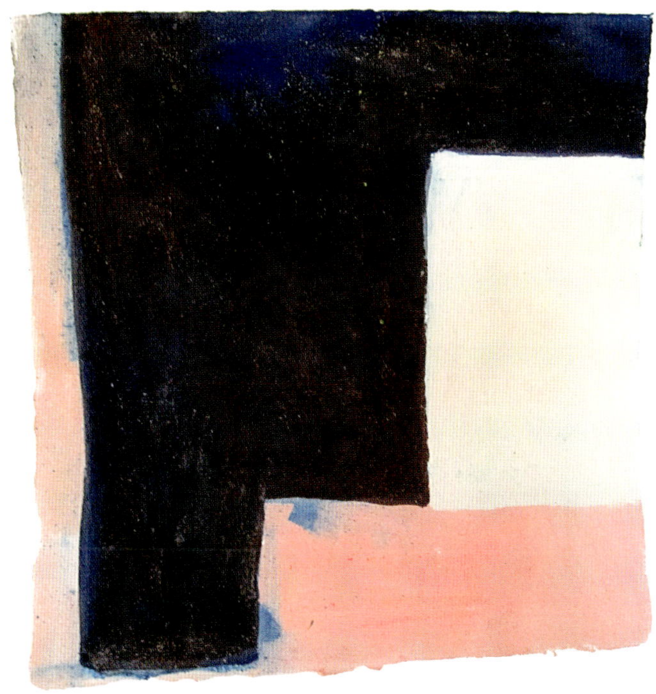

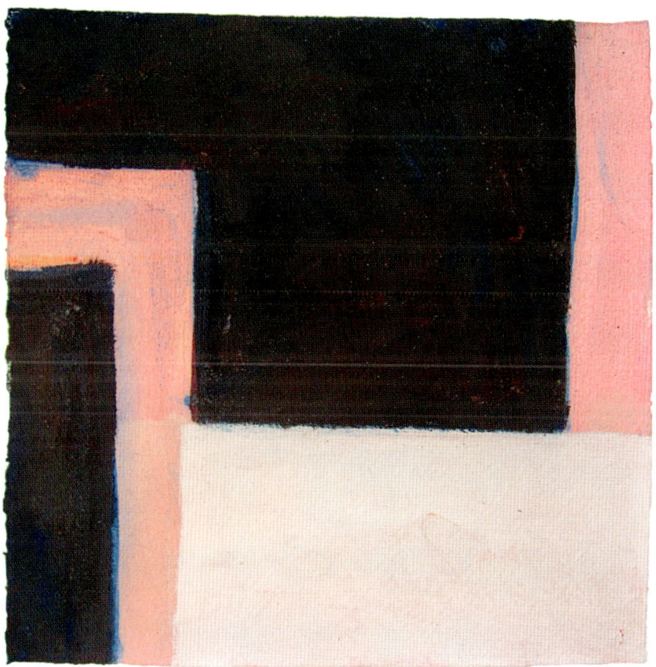

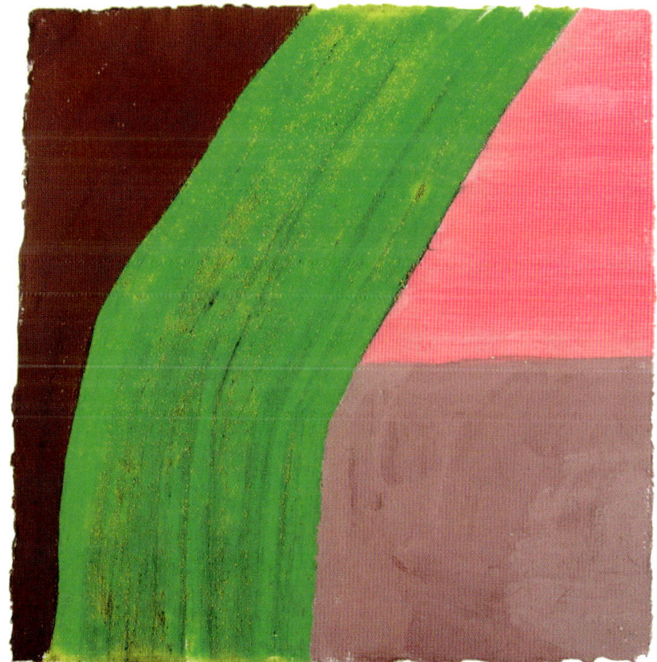

ABOVE:
Siteplan Marrakech, 2012
Egg tempera | Pigment | Handmade paper
7.9 x 7.9 in. | 20 x 20 cm

BELOW:
Siteplan Marrakech, 2012
Egg tempera | Pigment | Handmade paper
7.9 x 7.9 in. | 20 x 20 cm
Private collection

ABOVE:
Siteplan Marrakech, 2012
Egg tempera | Pigment | Handmade paper
7.9 x 7.9 in. | 20 x 20 cm
Private collection

BELOW:
Siteplan Marrakech, 2012
Egg tempera | Pigment | Handmade paper
7.9 x 7.9 in. | 20 x 20 cm
Private collection

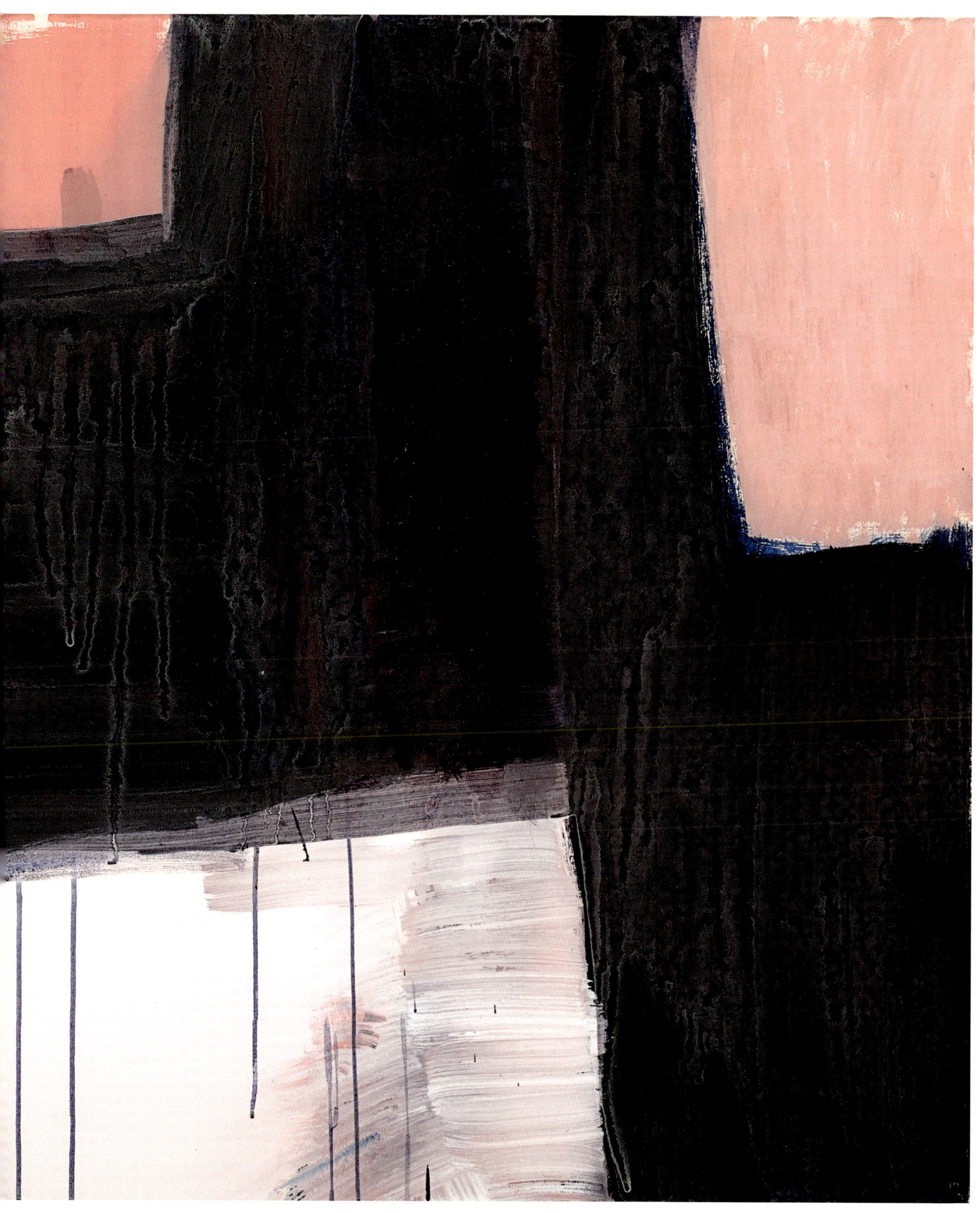

Siteplan Marrakech, 2012
Acrylics | Pigment | Canvas
35.4 x 63 in. | 90 x 160 cm

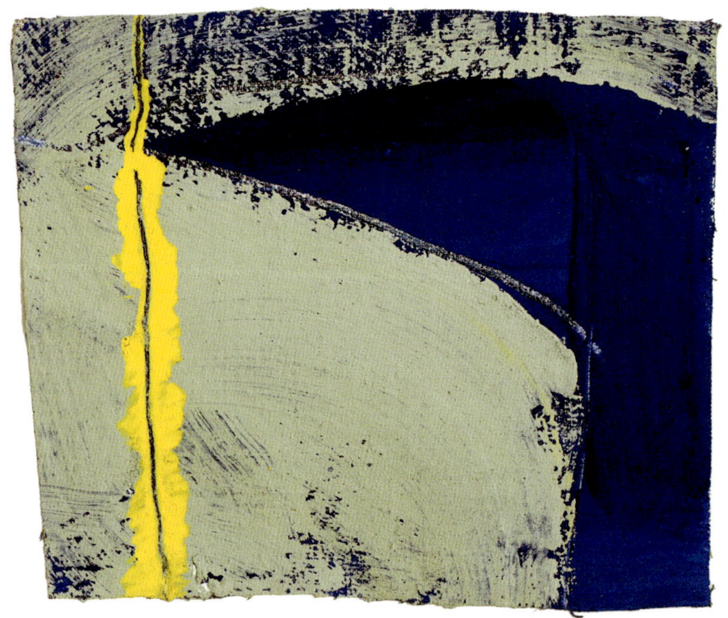

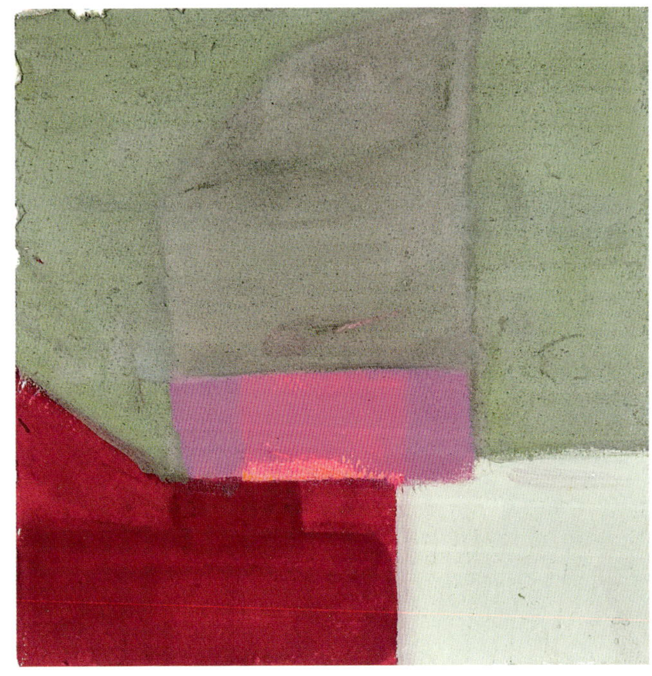

ABOVE:
Siteplan, 1994
Acrylics | Pigment | Canvas
7.5 x 8.3 in. | 19 x 21 cm
Private collection

BELOW:
Siteplan Würzburg, 2005
Egg tempera | Pigment | Handmade paper
7.9 x 7.9 in. | 20 x 20 cm
Private collection

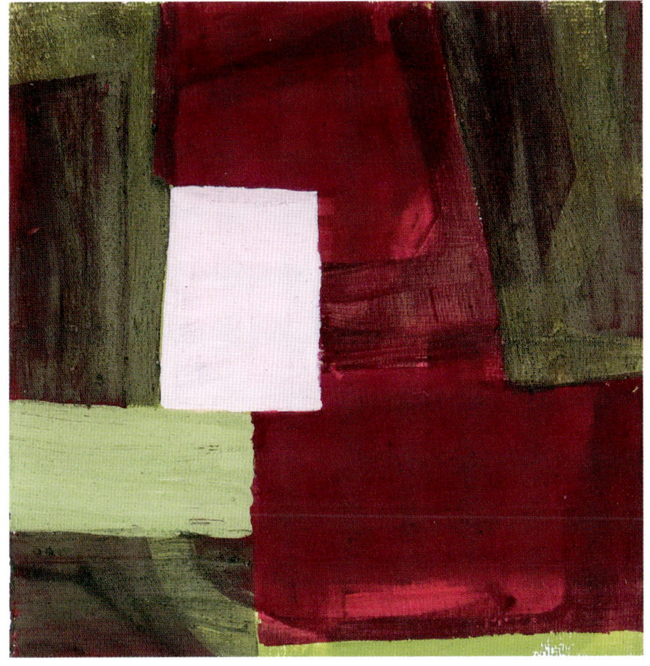

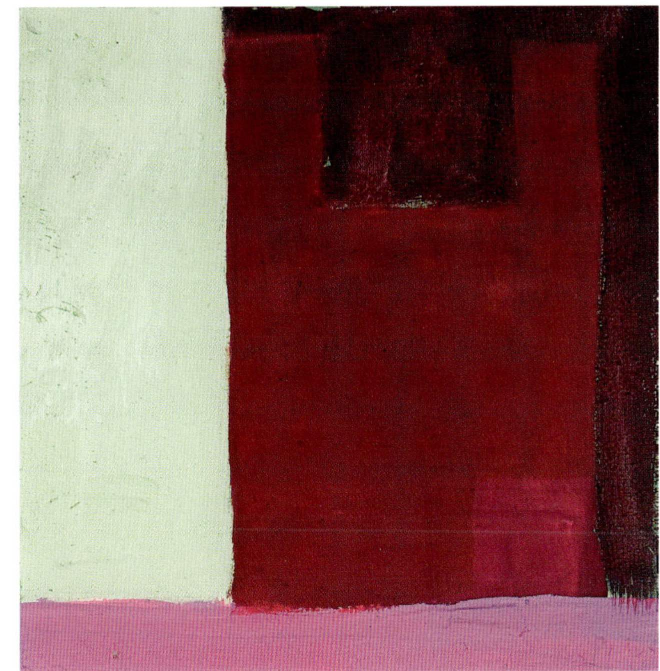

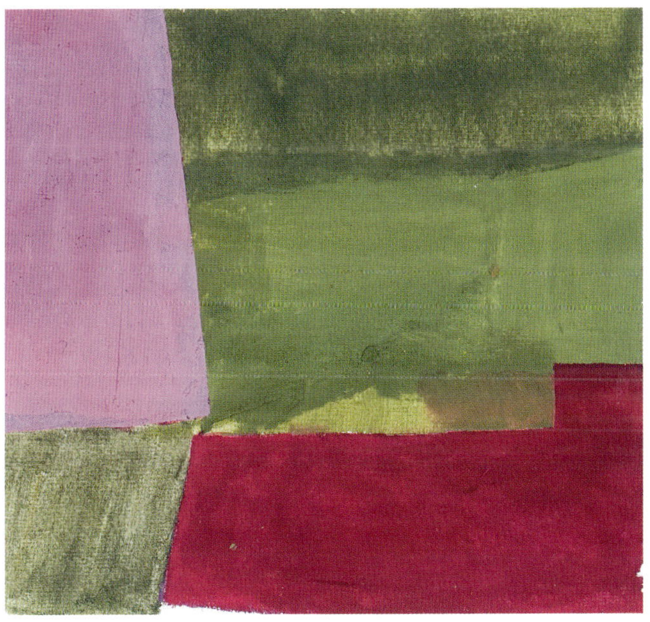

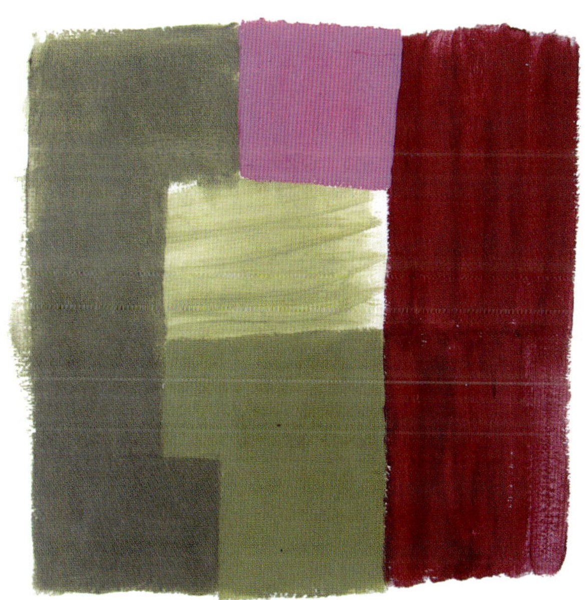

ABOVE:
Siteplan Würzburg, 2009
Egg tempera | Pigment | Handmade paper
7.9 x 7.9 in. | 20 x 20 cm

BELOW:
Siteplan Würzburg, 2009
Egg tempera | Pigment | Handmade paper
7.9 x 7.9 in. | 20 x 20 cm

ABOVE:
Siteplan Würzburg, 2009
Egg tempera | Pigment | Handmade paper
7.9 x 7.9 in. | 20 x 20 cm

BELOW:
Siteplan Würzburg, 2009
Egg tempera | Pigment | Handmade paper
7.9 x 7.9 in. | 20 x 20 cm

# Plätze

# Places

Klare Form

Umgrenzung

Umgebung

Innen und außen

Figur und Grund

clear form

perimeter

environment

inside and outside

figure and ground

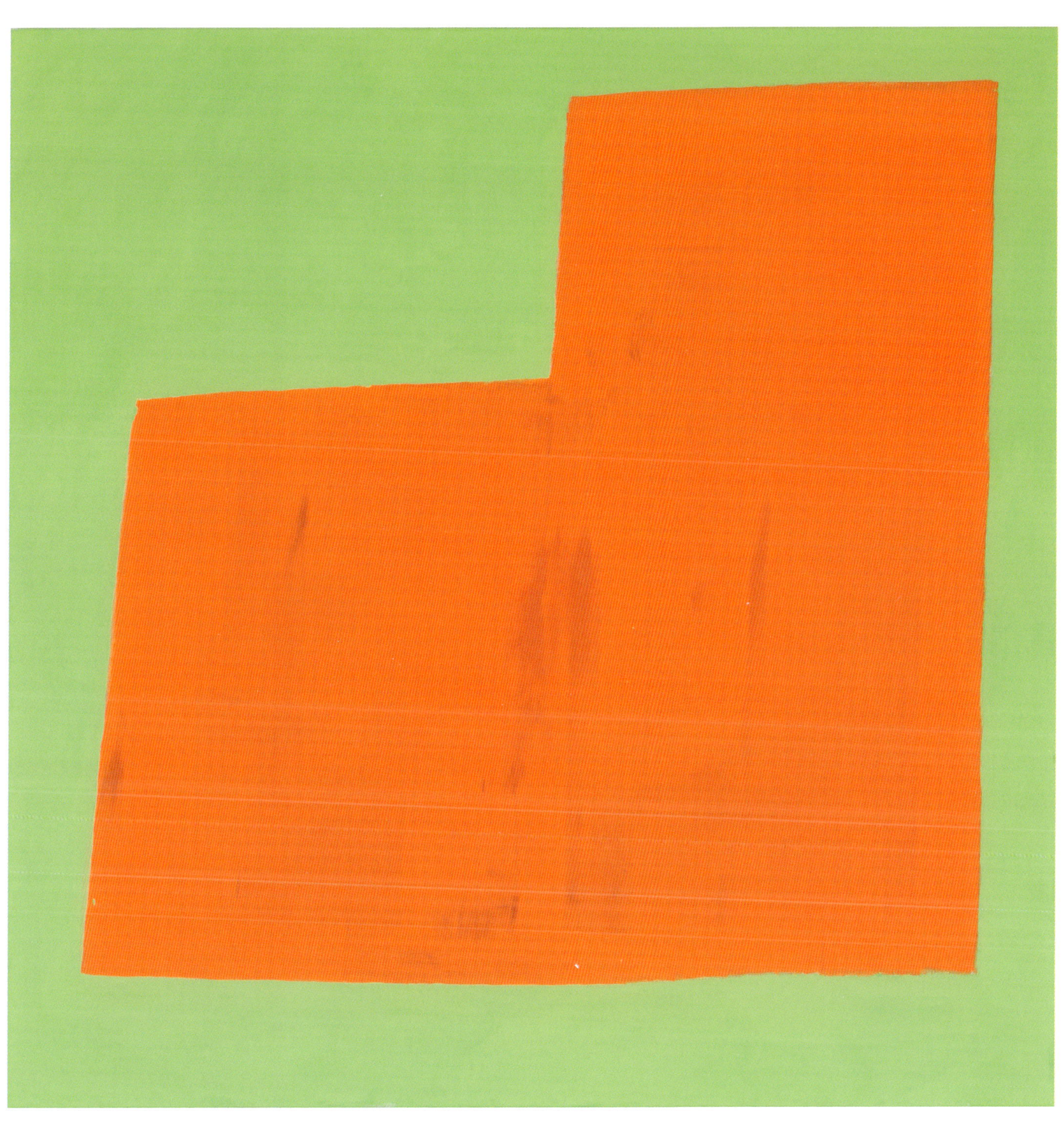

Siteplan Place Orange, 2012
Egg tempera | Pigment | Canvas
59 x 59 in. | 150 x 150 cm

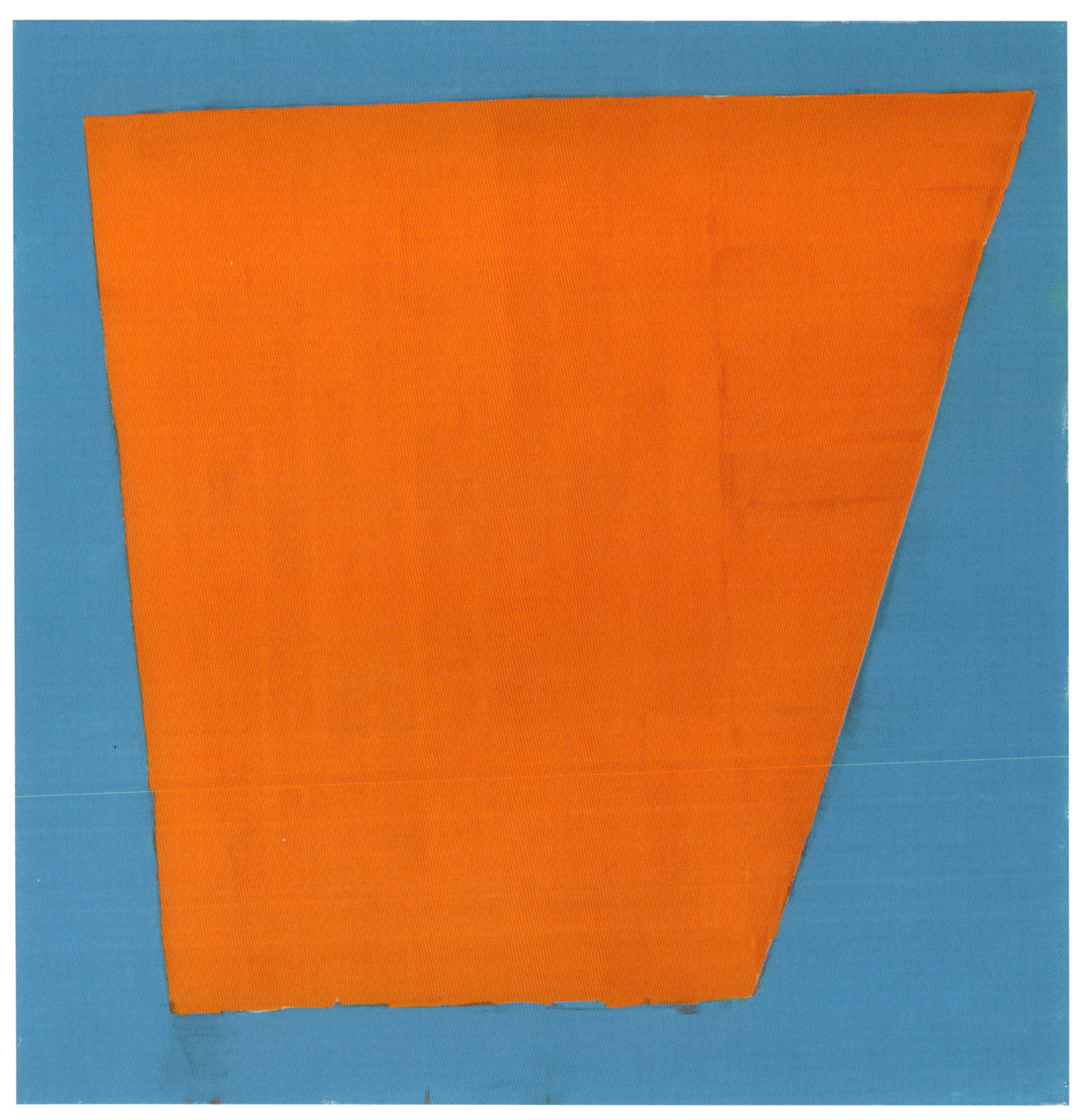

Siteplan Place Orange, 2012
Egg tempera | Pigment | Canvas
59 x 59 in. | 150 x 150 cm

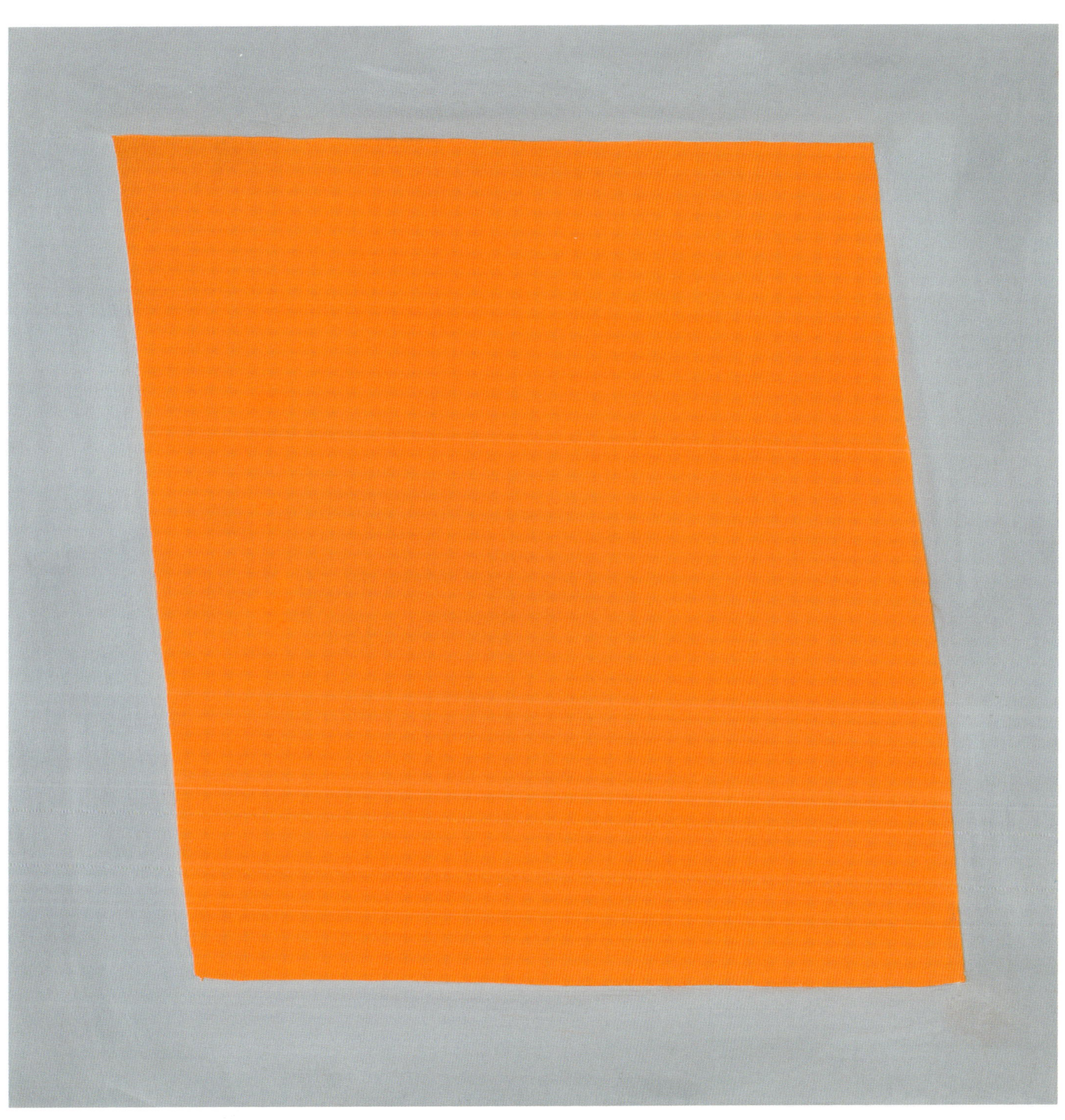

Siteplan Place Orange, 2012
Egg tempera | Pigment | Canvas
39.4 x 39.4 in. | 100 x 100 cm

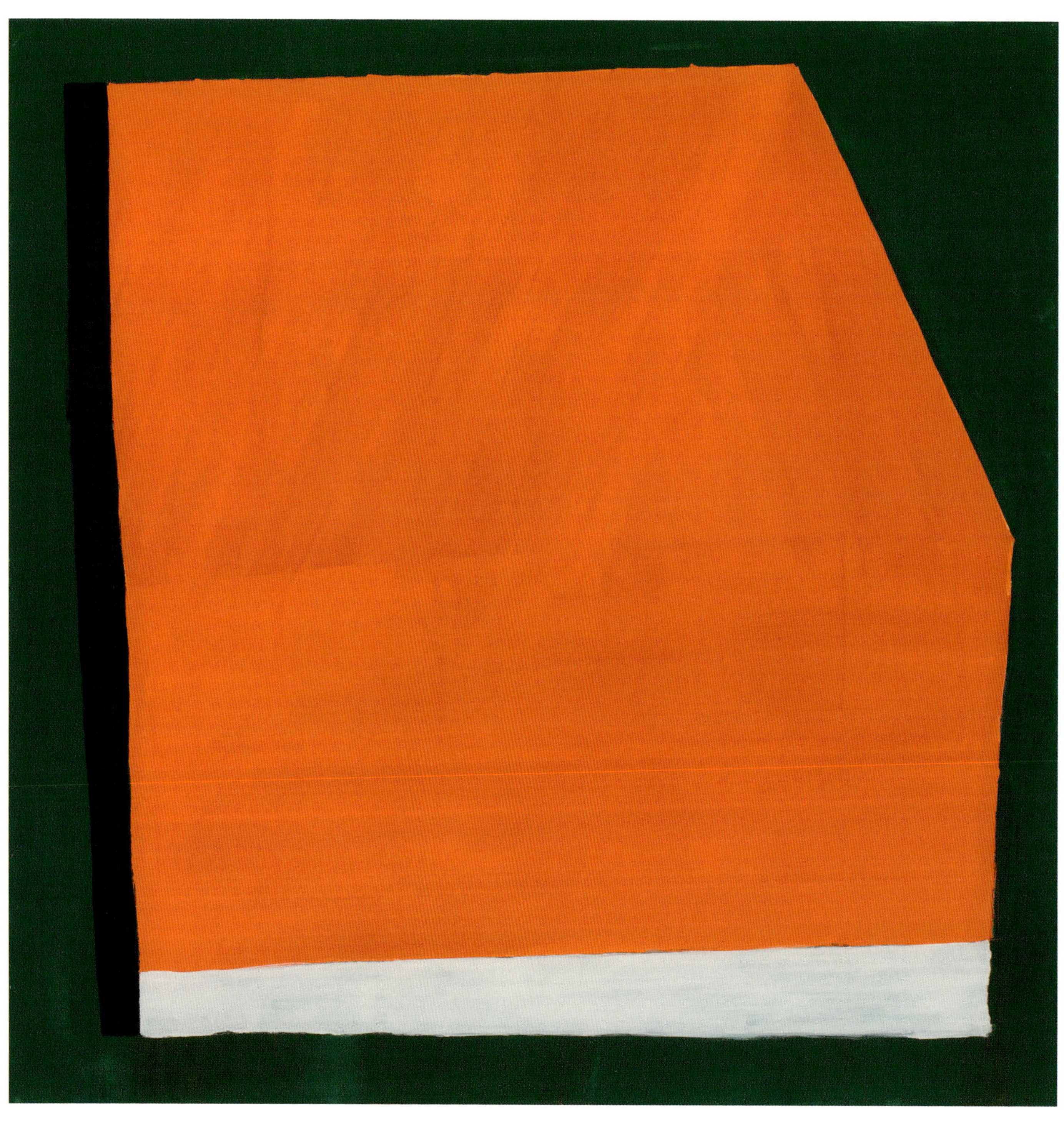

Siteplan Place Orange, 2012
Egg tempera | Pigment | Canvas
59 x 59 in. | 150 x 150 cm
Private collection

Siteplan Yellow Place, 2012
Acrylics | Pigment | Canvas
55.1 x 55.1 in. | 140 x 140 cm

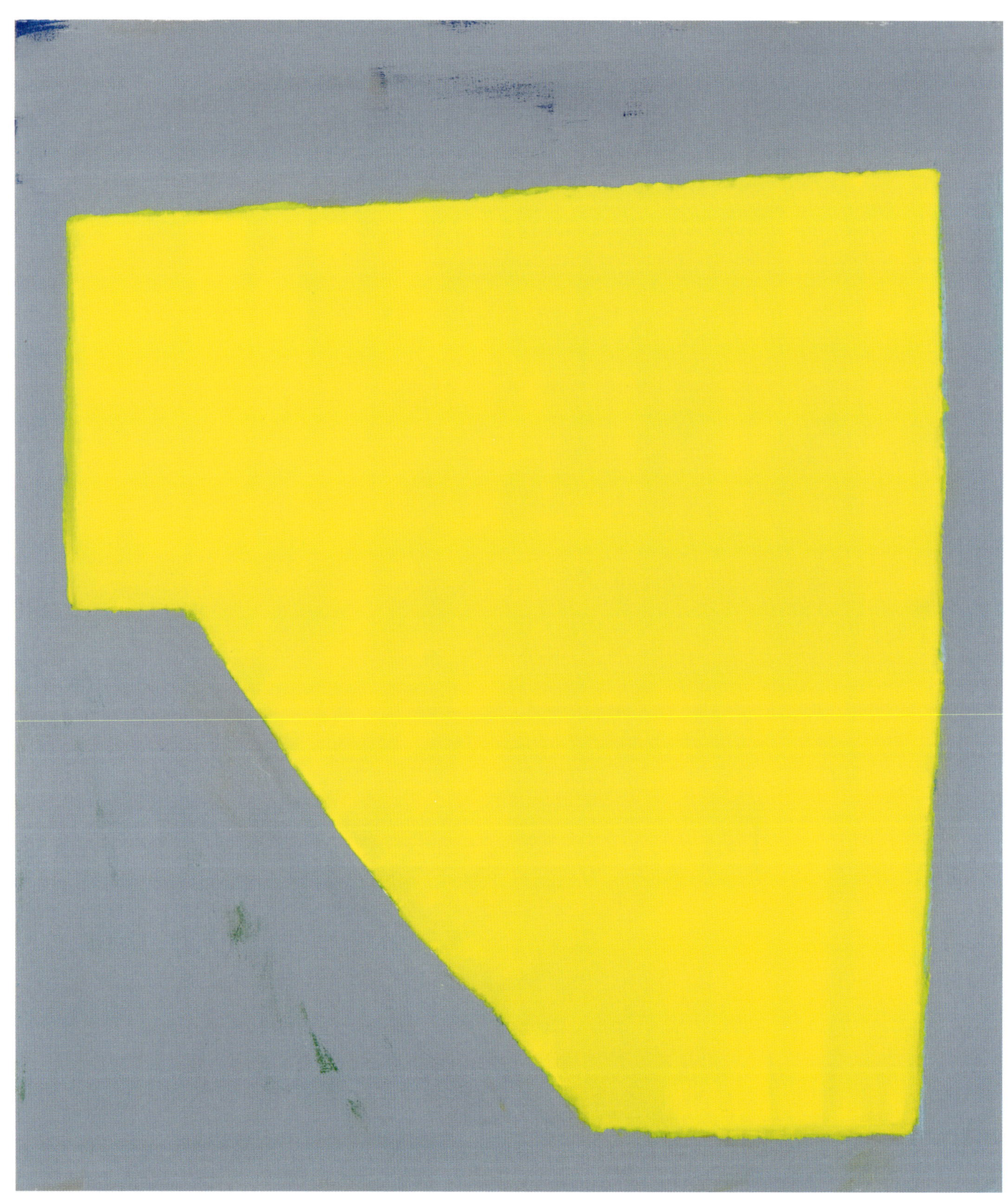

Siteplan Yellow Place, 2009
Acrylics | Pigment | Canvas
55.1 x 47.2 in. | 140 x 120 cm

Siteplan Yellow Place, 2009
Acrylics | Pigment | Canvas
55.1 x 47.2 in. | 140 x 120 cm

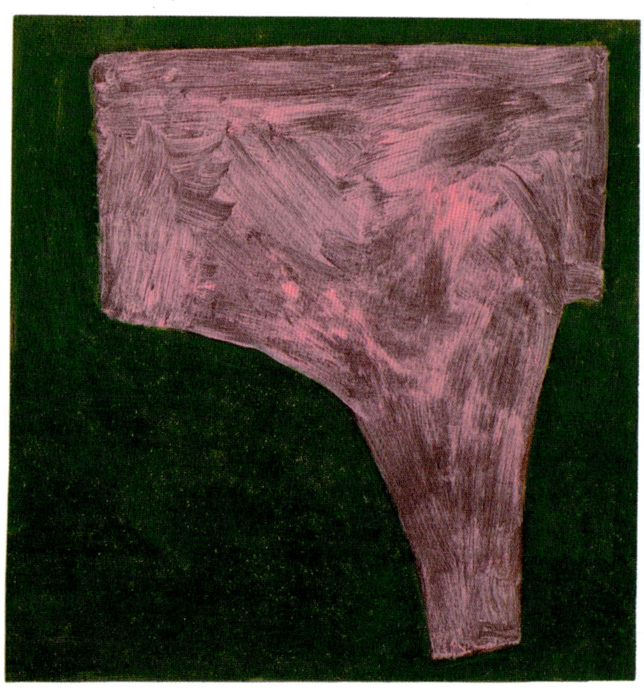

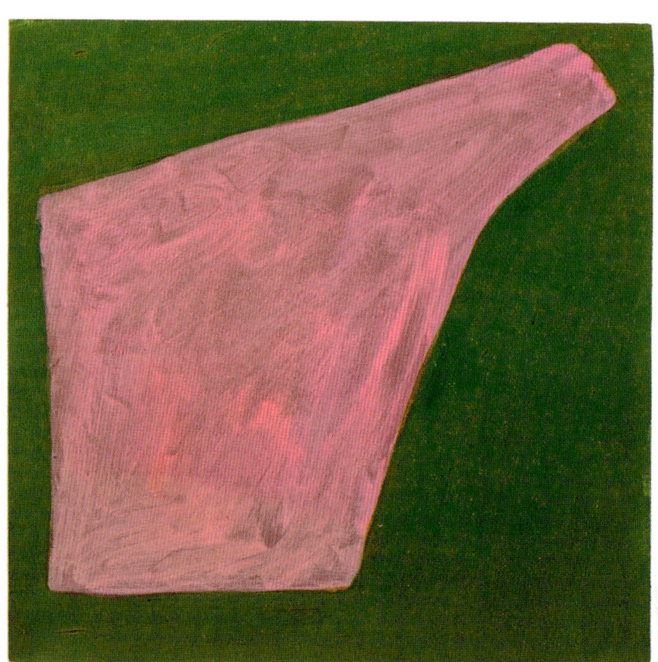

Siteplan Pink Place, 2013
Acrylics | Pigment | Paper
7.9 x 7.9 in. | 20 x 20 cm

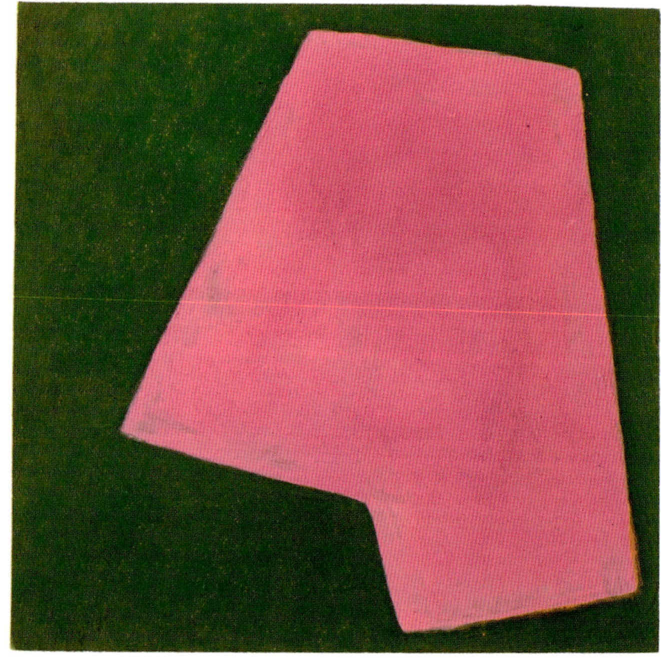

ABOVE:
Siteplan Pink Place, 2013
Acrylics | Pigment | Paper
7.9 x 7.9 in. | 20 x 20 cm

BELOW:
Siteplan Pink Place, 2013
Acrylics | Pigment | Paper
7.9 x 7.9 in. | 20 x 20 cm

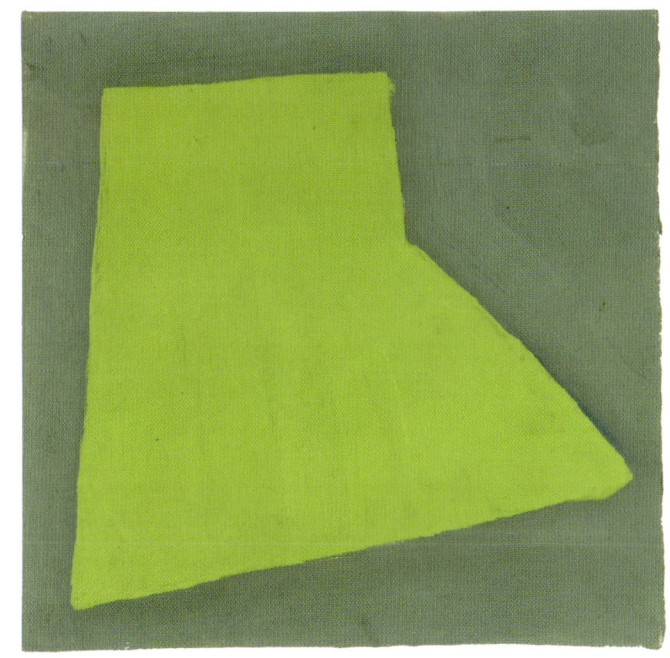

Siteplan Green Small, 2009
Egg tempera | Pigment | Paper
7.9 x 7.9 in. | 20 x 20 cm

ABOVE:
Siteplan Green Small, 2009
Egg tempera | Pigment | Paper
7.9 x 7.9 in. | 20 x 20 cm
Private collection

BELOW:
Siteplan Green Small, 2009
Egg tempera | Pigment | Paper
7.9 x 7.9 in. | 20 x 20 cm

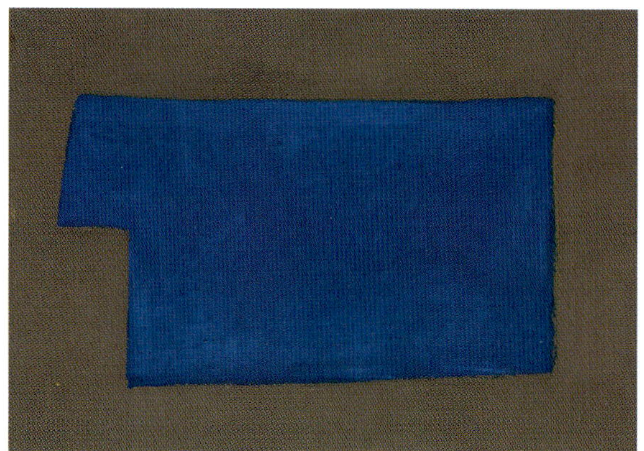

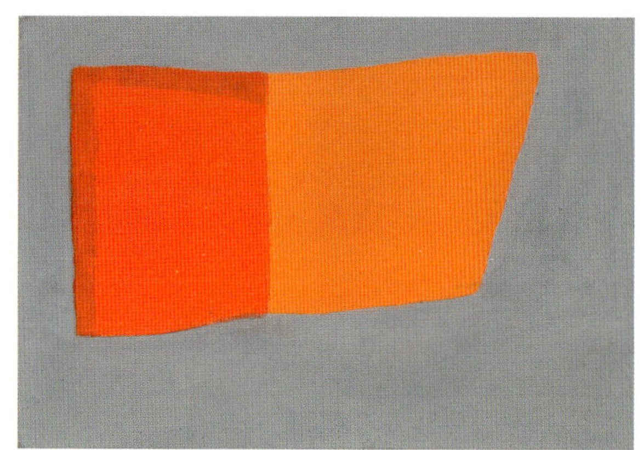

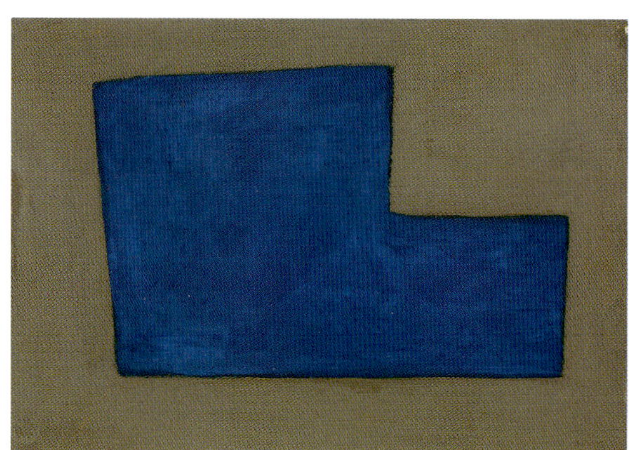

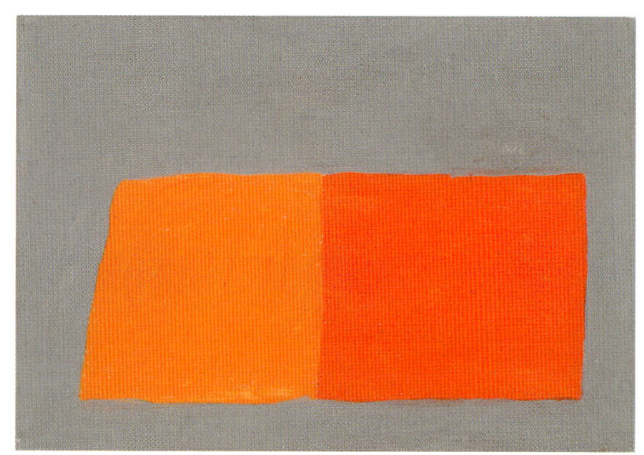

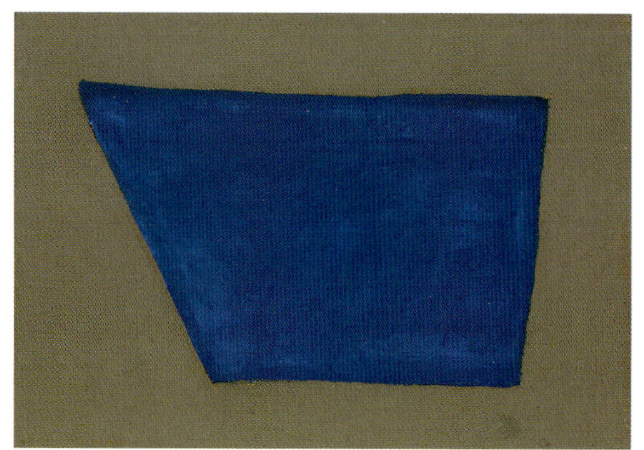

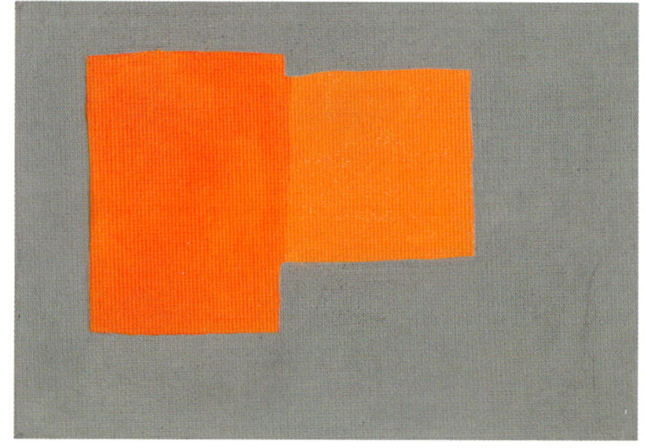

ABOVE:
Siteplan Blue Place, 2011
Egg tempera | Pigment | Wood
3.9 x 5.9 in. | 10 x 15 cm

MIDDLE:
Siteplan Blue Place, 2011
Egg tempera | Pigment | Wood
3.9 x 5.9 in. | 10 x 15 cm

BELOW:
Siteplan Blue Place, 2011
Egg tempera | Pigment | Wood
3.9 x 5.9 in. | 10 x 15 cm

ABOVE:
Siteplan Orange Place, 2011
Egg tempera | Pigment | Wood
3.9 x 5.9 in. | 10 x 15 cm

MIDDLE:
Siteplan Orange Place, 2011
Egg tempera | Pigment | Wood
3.9 x 5.9 in. | 10 x 15 cm

BELOW:
Siteplan Orange Place, 2011
Egg tempera | Pigment | Wood
3.9 x 5.9 in. | 10 x 15 cm

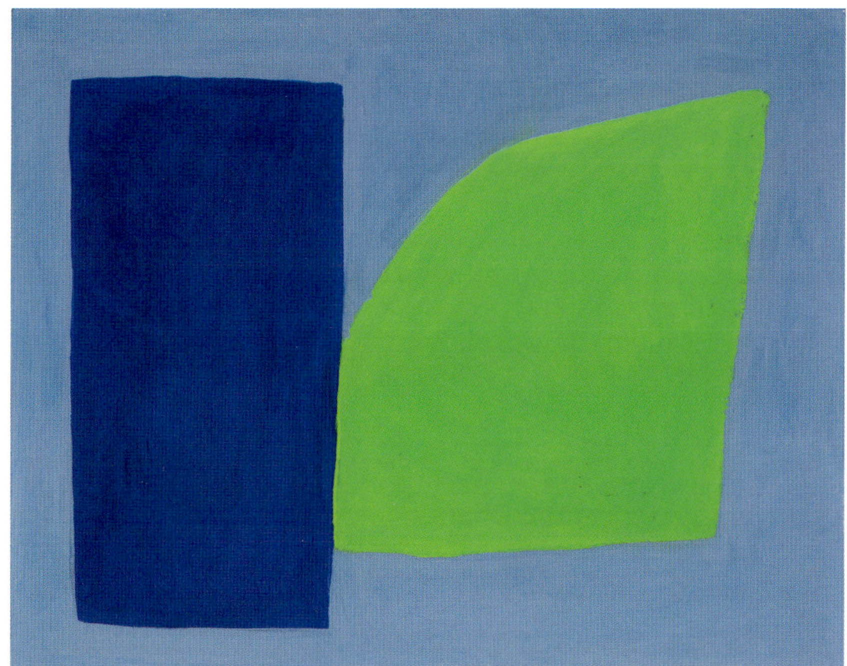

Siteplan Blue, Green, 2013
Egg tempera | Pigment | Wood
9 x 11.8 in. | 23 x 30 cm
Private collection

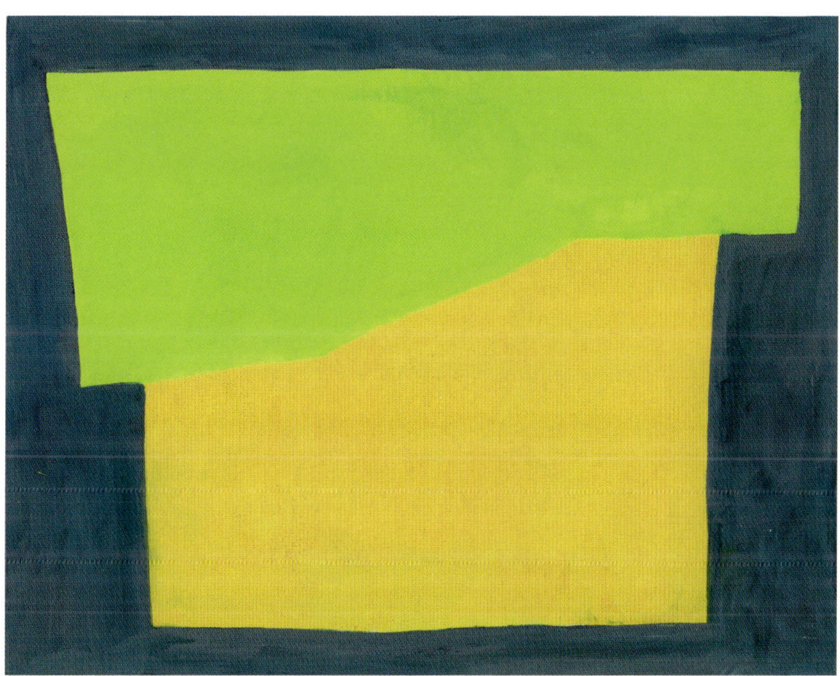

Siteplan, 2013
Egg tempera | Pigment | Wood
9 x 11.8 in. | 23 x 30 cm

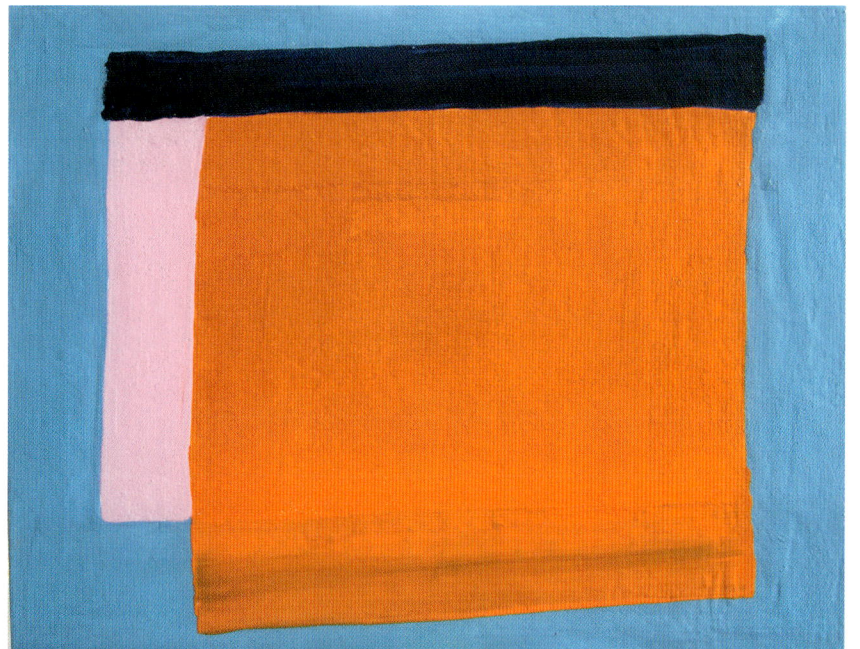

Siteplan Place Orange, 2013
Egg tempera | Pigment | Wood
9 x 11.8 in. | 23 x 30 cm

Siteplan Bulgaria, 2014
Egg tempera | Pigment | Handmade paper
24.8 x 24.8 in. | 63 x 63 cm

Siteplan Bulgaria, 2014
Egg tempera | Pigment | Handmade paper
24.8 x 24.8 in. | 63 x 63 cm

Siteplan Bulgaria, 2014
Egg tempera | Pigment | Handmade paper
24.8 x 24.8 in. | 63 x 63 cm

Siteplan Bulgaria, 2014
Egg tempera | Pigment | Handmade paper
24.8 x 24.8 in. | 63 x 63 cm

Siteplan Bulgaria, 2014
Egg tempera | Pigment | Handmade paper
24.8 x 24.8 in. | 63 x 63 cm

Siteplan Bulgaria, 2014
Egg tempera | Pigment | Handmade paper
24.8 x 24.8 in. | 63 x 63 cm

# Virginian Siteplans
## Malerei

Das Gespräch zwischen Wolfgang Hülsen und Elvira Lantenhammer wurde anlässlich ihrer Ausstellung auf der Arte Noah im Kunstverein Würzburg im Juni 2016 geführt.

**Wolfgang Hülsen:** Elvira Lantenhammer wurde in Altötting geboren. In den Jahren 1976 bis 1979 absolvierte sie eine Ausbildung zur Restauratorin.

Elvira, kannst du uns kurz schildern, weshalb du das Restaurieren aufgegeben hast und dich von1980 bis 1986 dem Studium der Malerei an der Akademie der Bildenden Künste in München gewidmet hast?

**Elvira Lantenhammer:** Meine Liebe und Bewunderung für die Kunst aus vergangenen Zeiten hat mich zum Restaurieren gebracht. Das Wiederherstellen von wunderbaren Werken aus dem Barock – Tafelbilder, gefasste Skulpturen, Fresken –, zum Teil in desolatem Zustand, war eine großartige Herausforderung. So war ich zum Beispiel beteiligt an der Restaurierung von St. Bartholomä am Königssee und der Fresken im Passauer Dom. Schließlich war der Wunsch, meine eigenen Kompositionen vor mir auszubreiten, so groß geworden, dass ich mich an der Kunstakademie in München bewarb.

**W. H.:** Du beschäftigst dich schon seit 1998 intensiv mit dem Thema „Lageplan". Die Werke, die dazu entstanden sind, sehen ja nicht aus wie Karten, sondern scheinen ein anderes malerisches Konzept zu verfolgen.

# Virginian Siteplans
## Paintings

Wolfgang Hülsen's conversation with Elvira Lantenhammer took place on the occasion of her exhibition at the Arte Noah in the Kunstverein Würzburg in June 2016

**Wolfgang Hülsen:** Elvira Lantenhammer was born in Altötting and trained as a restorer in the years 1976 to 1979.

Elvira, can you briefly tell us why you gave up restoring and devoted yourself to studying painting at the Academy of Fine Arts in Munich (from 1980 to 1986)?

**Elvira Lantenhammer:** My love and admiration for art from past times brought me to restoration. Restoring wonderful Gothic and Baroque works—panel paintings, framed sculptures, frescoes—partly in desolate condition, was a great challenge. For example, I was involved in the restoration of the church of St. Bartholomä at the lake of Königssee and the frescoes in Passau Ca-thedral. But eventually, the desire to spread out my own compositions in front of me had become so great, that I applied to the Academy of Fine Arts in Munich.

**W. H.:** Since 1998, you have been engaged intensively in the subject "Siteplan." The resulting works do not look like maps at all, but seem to pursue a different artistic concept. How did you conceive this idea and what is the reasoning behind it? And can you give a short explana-

Wie bist du auf die Idee gekommen und welche Bewandtnis hat es damit? Und kannst du deinen Ansatz am Beispiel der „Virginian Siteplans", die 2015 in den USA entstanden sind kurz erläutern?

**E. L.:** Der Impuls, meinen abstrakten Kompositionen den Titel „Lagepläne" zu geben, kam, als ich in den entstandenen Werken im Atelier selbst Blicke auf Formationen, Anlagen von Orten, Plätzen, völlig frei, nach der Fantasie, entdeckte. Dann interessierte es mich, wie ich mit Farben auf konkrete Orte reagiere und was daraus entsteht, welche Bilder dadurch hervorgebracht werden.

Auf Spaziergängen, Wanderungen, Ausflügen um den Barn Complex, San Angelo Drive 154, erkundete ich den Ort und die weitere Region mit dem Skizzenbuch. Die mitgebrachten Schattenformen inspirierten mich zu Malereien mit leuchtendem Gelb. Parallel zu den Erkundungen experimentierte ich mit Farben. Schließlich entwickelte sich der Farbklang, der für mich stimmte.

tion, with the "Virginian Siteplans," created in the USA in 2015, as an example?

**E.L.:** The impulse to give my abstract compositions the title "Siteplans" was released, when I discovered in the completed works in my studio views of formations, structures of places, squares, completely free, without any association, only following my imagination. Then I became interested in how I react with colors to con-crete places, and what results from it, which pictures are produced by it.

On walks, hikes, excursions around the Barn Complex, San Angelo Drive 154, I explored the location and the wider region by making sketches. The shadow forms I captured inspired me to paint with a bright yellow color. Parallel to these excursions, I started to experiment with colors. Finally, the color tone, which seemed right for me, developed.

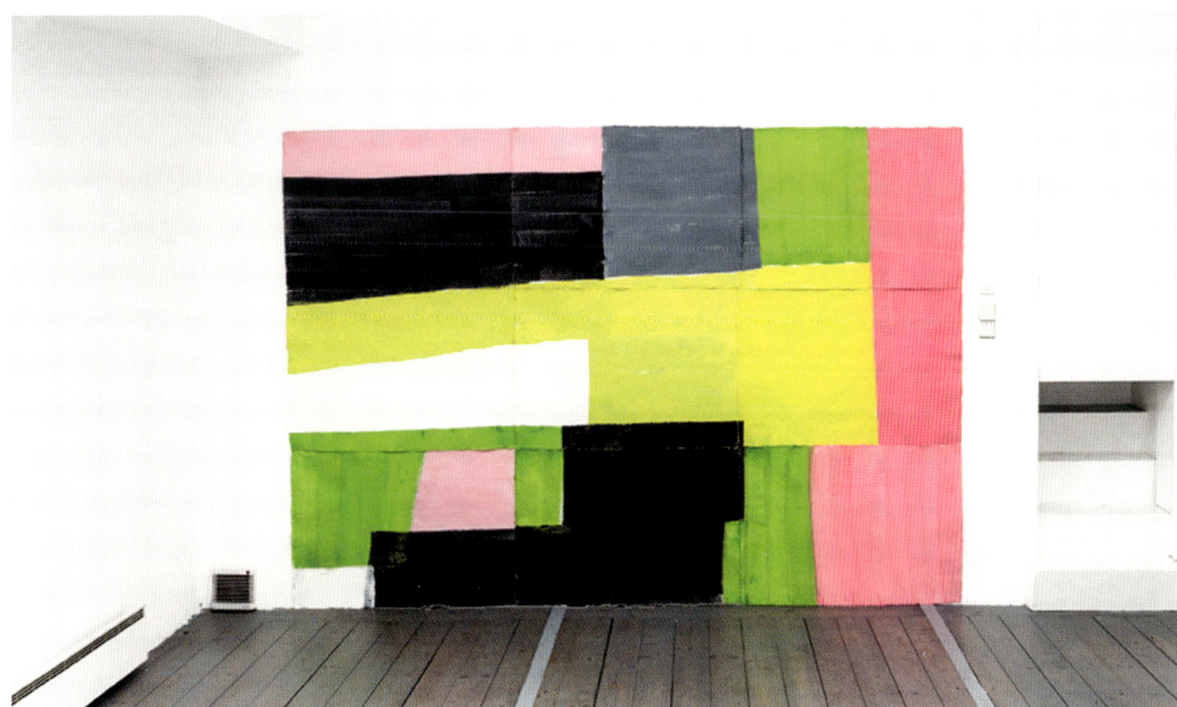

Virginian Siteplan
Installation 2016
Kunstverein Würzburg

Alle Arbeiten sind in der Technik Eitempera / Pigment / Himalaya-Büttenpapier ausgeführt. Das bedeutet, dass ich morgens damit beschäftigt war, in einem sehr aufwendigen Prozedere die Farbsubstanzen nach einem alten Rezept anzurühren und herzustellen. Mein Verbrauch an „Amherst Bio Eggs" war immens! Nachmittags malte ich damit auf Himalaya-Büttenpapier meine Kompositionen. Die großen Bögen dieses speziellen Papiers hatte ich im Vorfeld per Post nach USA gesendet.

All works were technically executed in egg tempera / pigment / Himalaya handmade paper. This meant to me to be busy in the morning, mixing, in a very complex procedure, the color substances according to an old recipe. My consumption of "Amherst Bio Eggs" was immense! In the afternoon, I used the mixture to paint my compositions on Himalayan handmade paper. I had, in advance, sent the large sheets of this special paper to the USA by post.

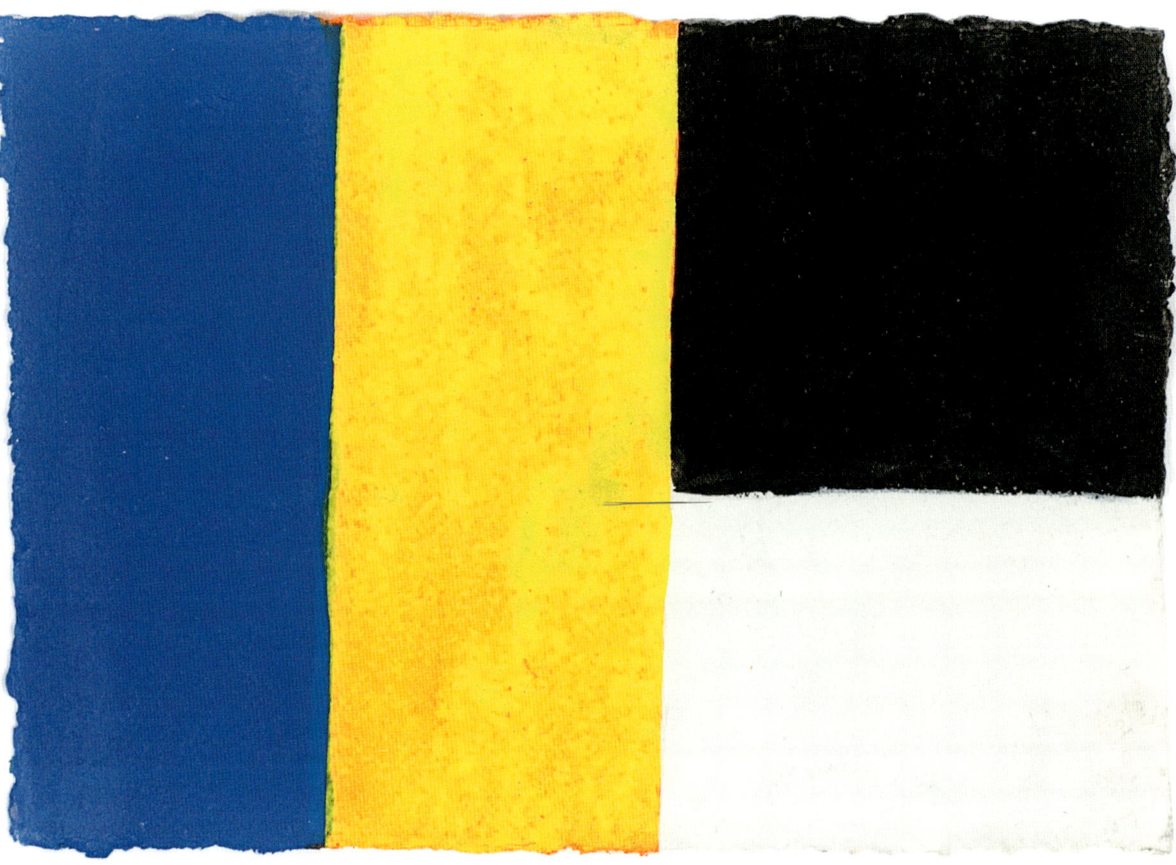

San Angelo Drive 4, 2015
Egg tempera | Pigment | Handmade paper
9.8 x 13.3 in. | 25 x 34 cm

**W. H.:** Die Malereien sind streng kalkulierte Bildkonstruktionen, deren Formen einerseits den Rahmen bilden für eine rein malerische Formulierung, wobei die Farbwerte räumlich gestaffelt sind oder flach nebeneinanderliegen. Doch wenn ich mir die „Lagepläne" genau betrachte, finde ich keinen Hinweis auf Straßen, Plätze oder Parks, mit deren Hilfe ich mich orientieren könnte

**W. H.:** The paintings are strictly composed, their elements providing the framework for a purely painterly formulation, whereby the color values lie spatially staggered or flat next to each other. But when I look closely at the "Siteplans," there are no reference points like streets, squares, or parks to realign.

**E. L.:** Für mich sind die Bilder auch Seelenlandschaften, in denen ich meine innere Stimmung und Empfindungen über die Örtlichkeit in Farben ausdrücke. Diese Empfindungen wie Landschaftseindrücke, Gerüche, Geräusche, Ideen und so weiter werden durch entsprechende Farben in kräftigem Rosa, Gelb, Weiß, Grün oder Schwarz umgesetzt. So antworten die „Virginian Siteplans" auf die Örtlichkeit und beziehen durch die malerische Anordnung ihre Spannung.

Gelb zuerst. Grün könnte stehen für die üppige Natur, auch die alles überwuchernde, aus Japan eingeführte Kudzu-Pflanze, die prallen, gelbgrünen, von allen, Mensch und Tier, als Nahrung verschmähten Monkey Brain Fruits. Das Rosa: die Liebe zum Kindlichen, „the American Way of Life", aber auch das Land der unbegrenzten Möglichkeiten, Donald Duck und Daisy, aber auch Facelifting und Marylin Monroe. Schwarz: die heftigen Brüche inmitten all der Heiterkeit, Abstürze, die abgrundtiefen Kontraste in der Gesellschaft.

**W. H.:** Das äußerlich Erkennbare und das subjektiv Bedeutsame, beides zusammengesehen, belegen erst die komplexe Vielfalt künstlerischer Erfahrung und Erkenntnis. Dabei ist zu bedenken, dass du als Künstlerin anders interpretierst als

**E. L.:** To me the pictures are also landscapes of the soul, they express the powerful emotions, which were caused by the locations and places I chose. These sensations, originating in the inspiring landscape impressions, smells, noises, ideas, are rendered by appropriate colors of strong pink, yellow, white, green, or black. This is how the "Virginian Siteplans" respond to the location and draw their tension from the painterly arrangement.

Yellow first. Green could stand for the luxuriant nature, including the originally Japanese Kudzu plant, which overgrows everything, and the bulging, yellow-green monkey-brain fruits, spurned as food by every creature. Pink: the love for the childlike, "the American Way of Life," but also the land of plenty, Donald Duck and Daisy, but also face-lifts and Marilyn Monroe. Black: the violent fractures in the midst of all the cheerfulness, crashes, the profound contrasts in society.

**W. H.:** Both, the outwardly recognizable and the subjectively significant—both seen together—only prove the complex diversity of artistic experience and knowledge. It should be borne in mind, that you, as the artist,

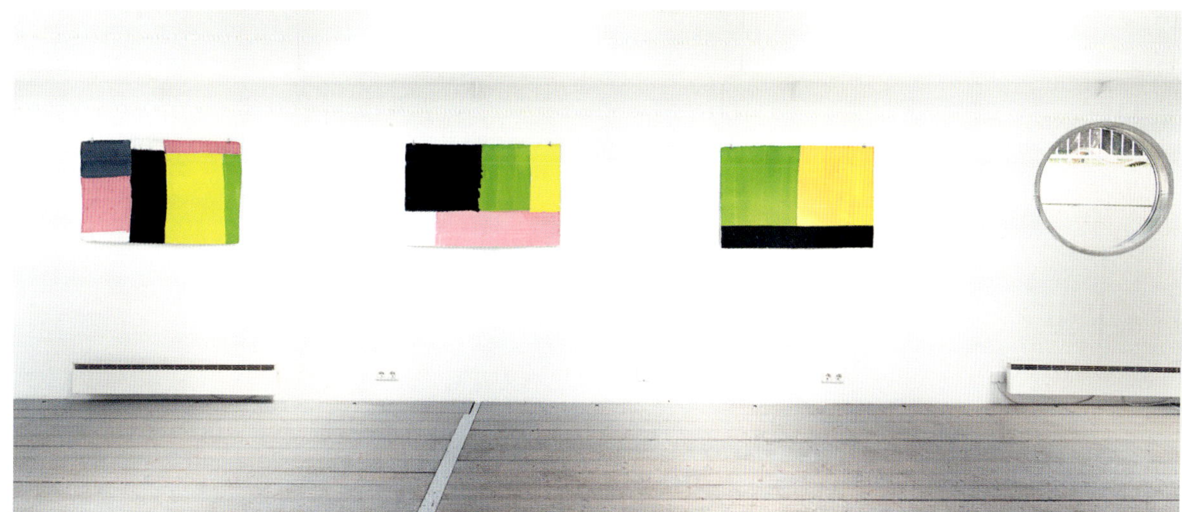

Virginian Siteplan
Installation 2016
Kunstverein Würzburg

der Betrachter. Dieses ambivalente Verhältnis von außen und innen lässt sich begrifflich schwer festlegen, wohl aber lässt es sich umkreisen oder andeutend erfahren. So wird der Beschauer selbst zum Gestalter einer eigenen Gedankenwelt, die auf das Gesehene Bezug nimmt.

Abschließend kann man sagen, dass die „Landschaftspläne" im Laufe der Zeit stringenter geworden sind und die Qualität der Farbabstufungen zugenommen hat.

**E. L.** Mit „Lageplänen" zeige ich, wie ich mich mit anderen Orten konfrontiere, mein Erleben in der Fremde sammle und nutzbar mache, es in Form von Bildern von einem Ort zum anderen transportiere und so wie hier in der Ausstellung „Virginian Siteplan", interagierend mit anderen Kunstformen, dem Betrachter in verschiedenen Kontexten die visuellen Eindrücke und Emotionen von Orten nahebringe. Es freut mich, dass man diese Bezüge in meinen Bildern sehen kann.

**interpret differently than the viewer. This ambivalent relationship between outside and inside is difficult to define conceptually, but it can be orbited or experienced in a suggestive way. Thus the viewer himself becomes the designer of his own thought world, which refers to what he has seen.**

**In conclusion, one can say that the "landscape plans" have become more compelling over the course of time and the quality of the color gradations has increased.**

**E. L.: With the "Siteplans" I show how I confront myself with other places, collect and utilize my experience of the foreign, transport it in the form of paintings from one place to the other, and, as in this exhibition "Virgin-ian Siteplan," interacting with other art forms, making the visual impressions and emotions of places accessible to the viewer in different contexts. I am delighted that these connections can be seen.**

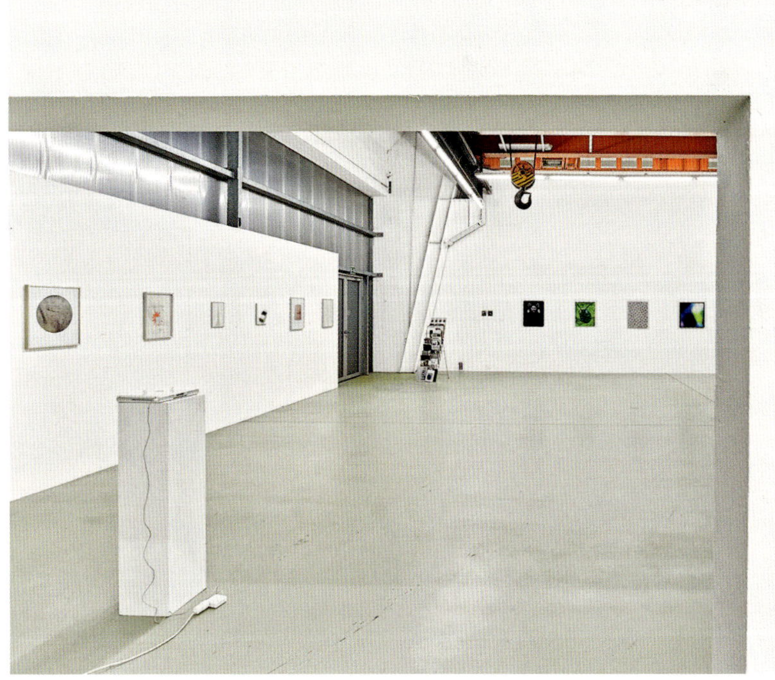
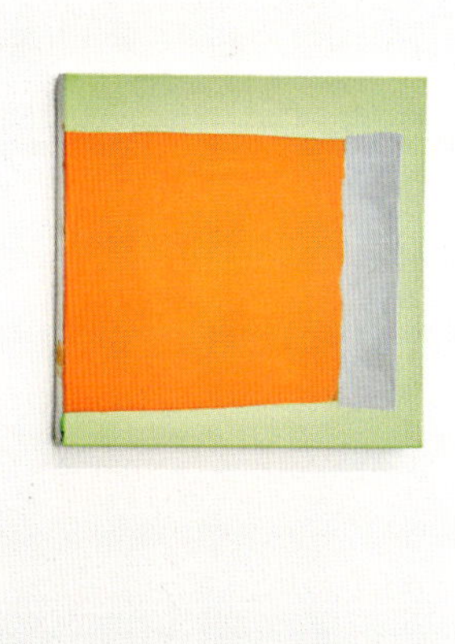

Siteplan Harbour, 2018
Domestic Space Domagk Edition
Halle 50, Munich

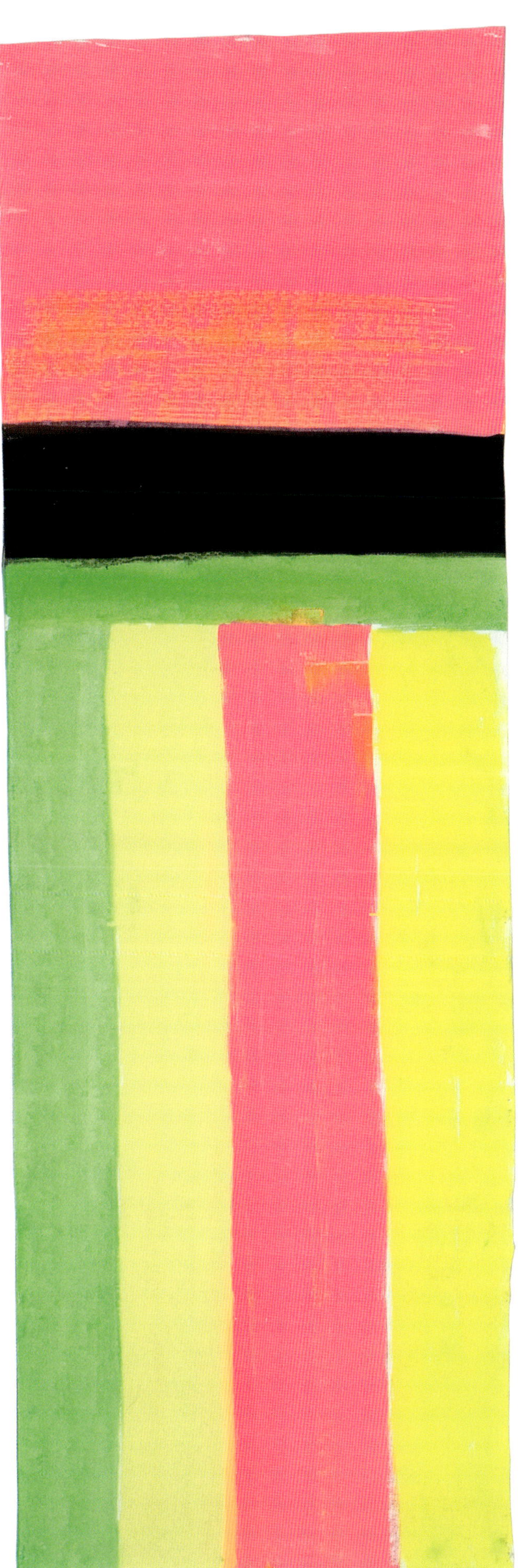

Virginian Siteplan, 2015
Egg tempera | Pigment | Canvas
62.9 x 11 in. | 160 x 28 cm

# Zusammengesetzte Werke Compound Works

Ausdehnung, fortsetzen, weiter ... expansion, continue, further ...

Größerer Zusammenhang greater context

Großzügigkeit generosity

Von Farbe umgeben sein be surrounded by color

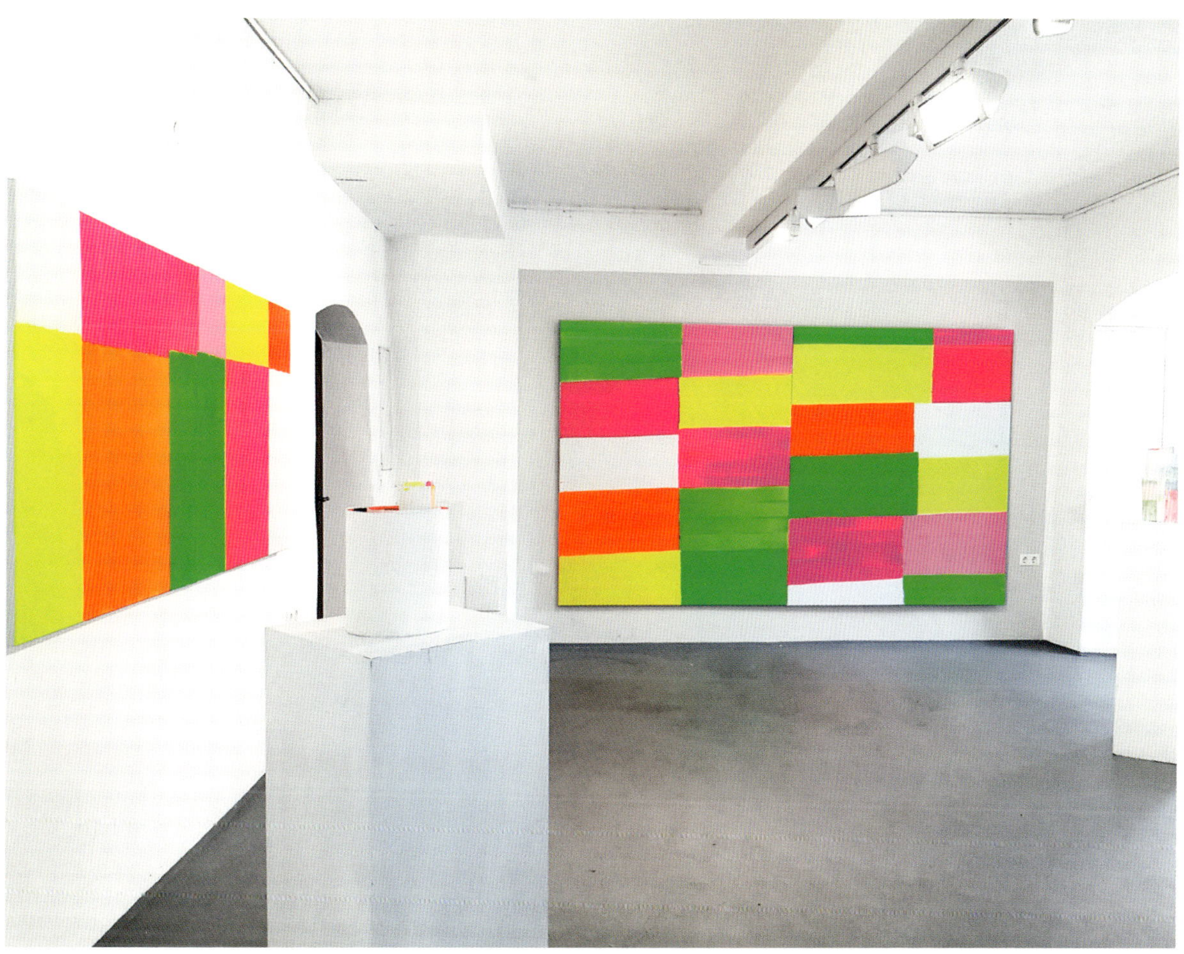

Japanese Siteplan
Installation 2019
Deutschordensschloss Münnerstadt

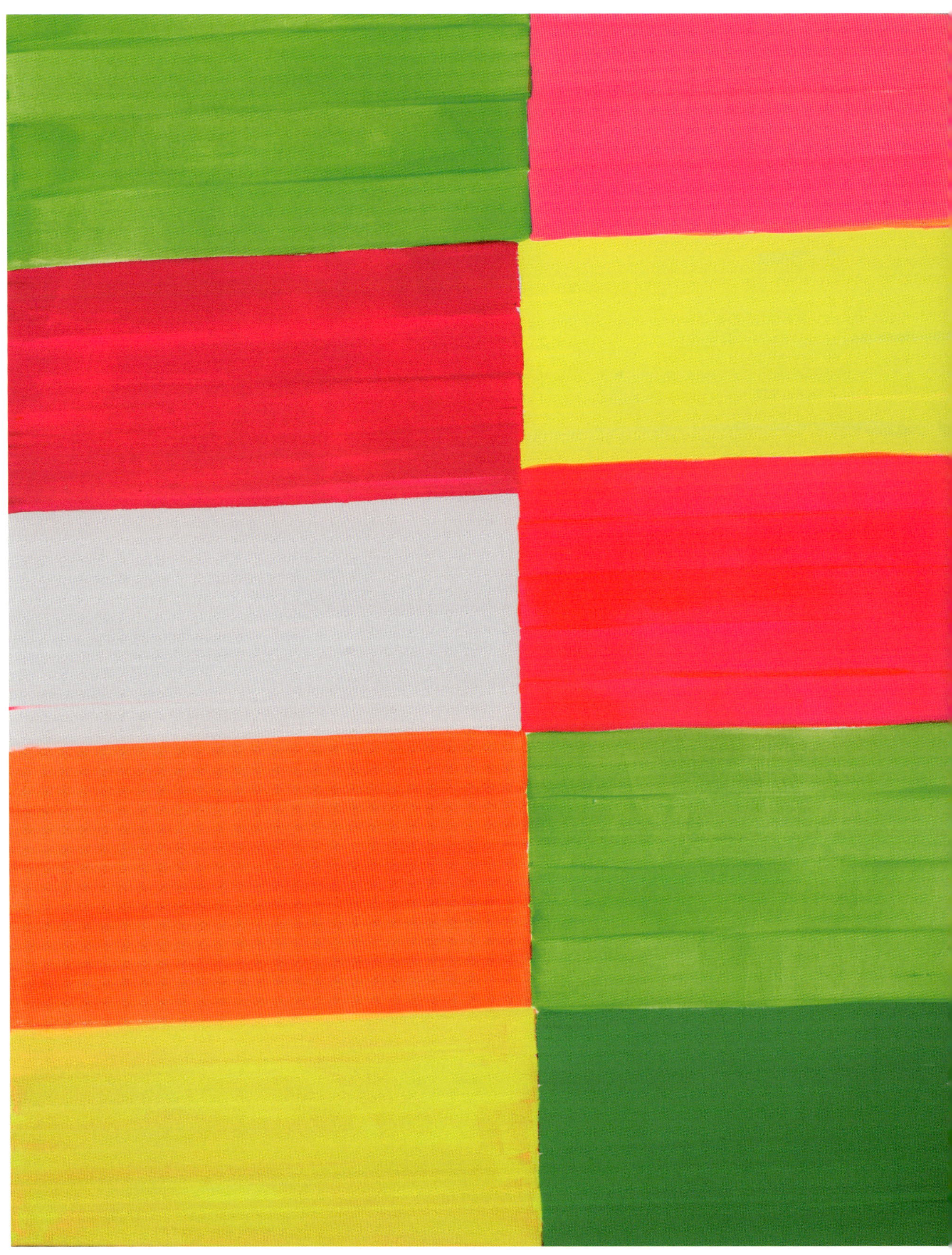

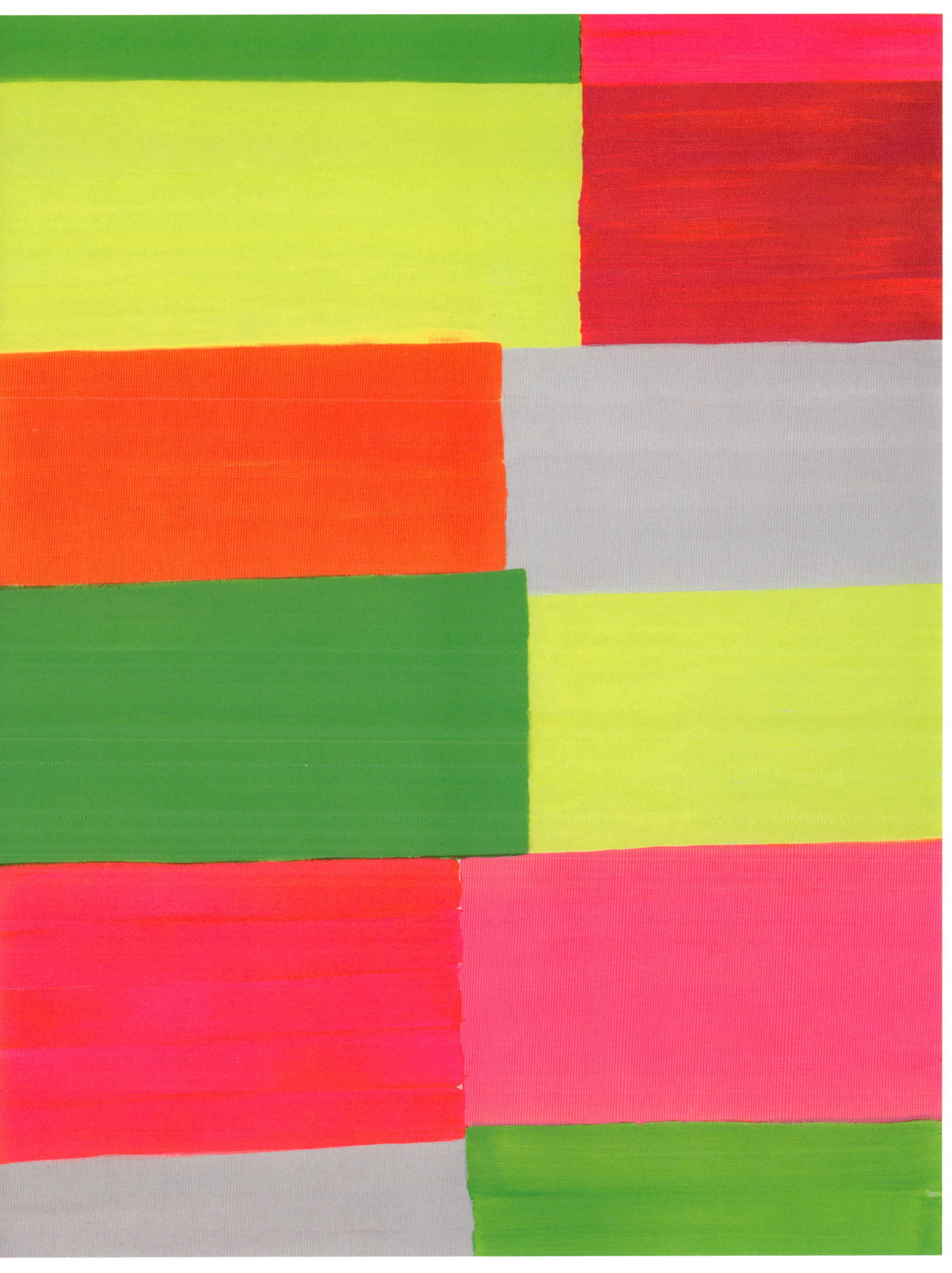

Japanese Siteplan, 2019
Diptych
Acrylics | Pigment | Canvas
74.8 x 126 in. | 190 x 320 cm

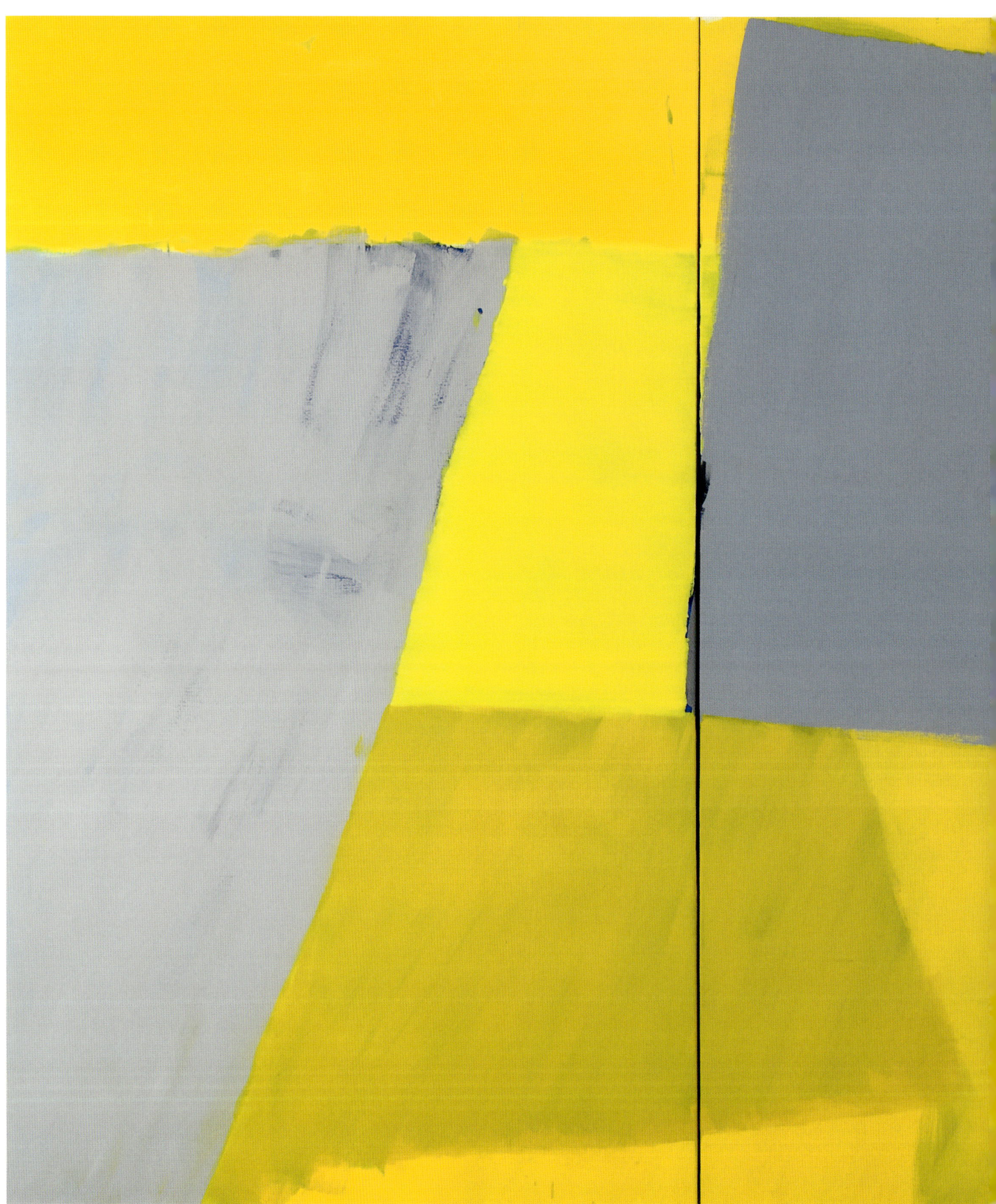

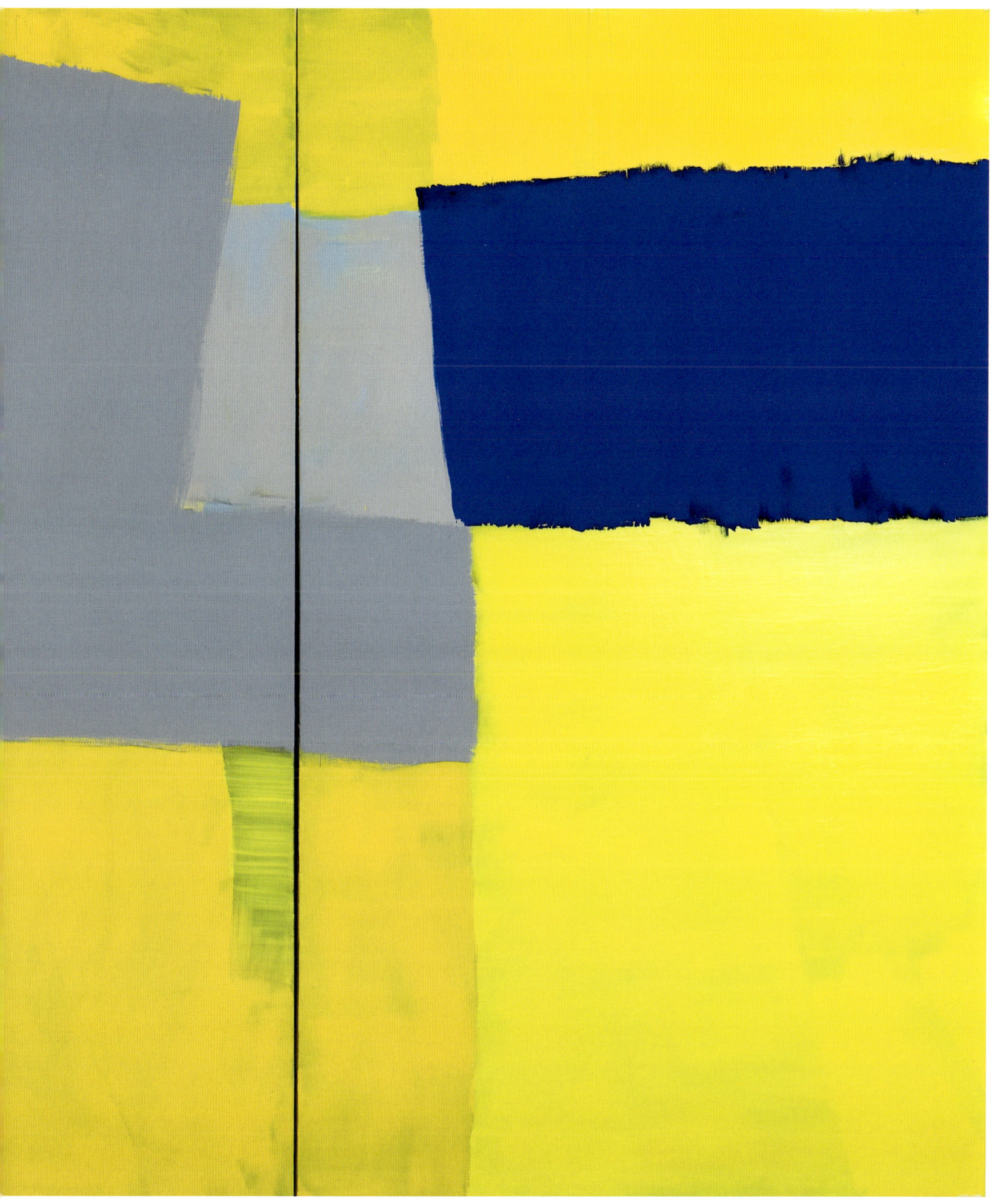

Siteplan Studio, 2009
Triptych
Acrylics | Pigment | Canvas
78.7 x 141.7 in. | 200 x 360 cm

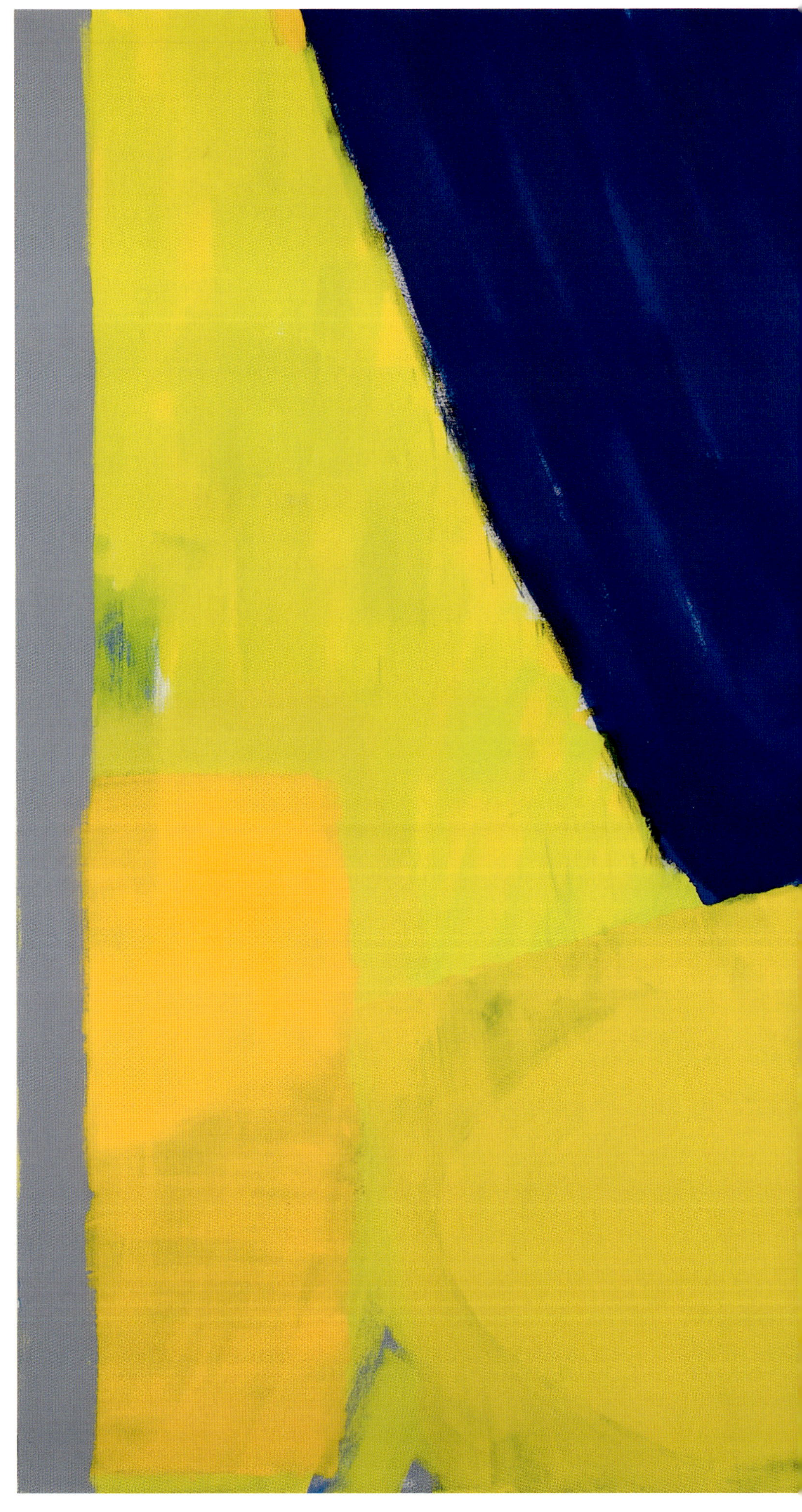

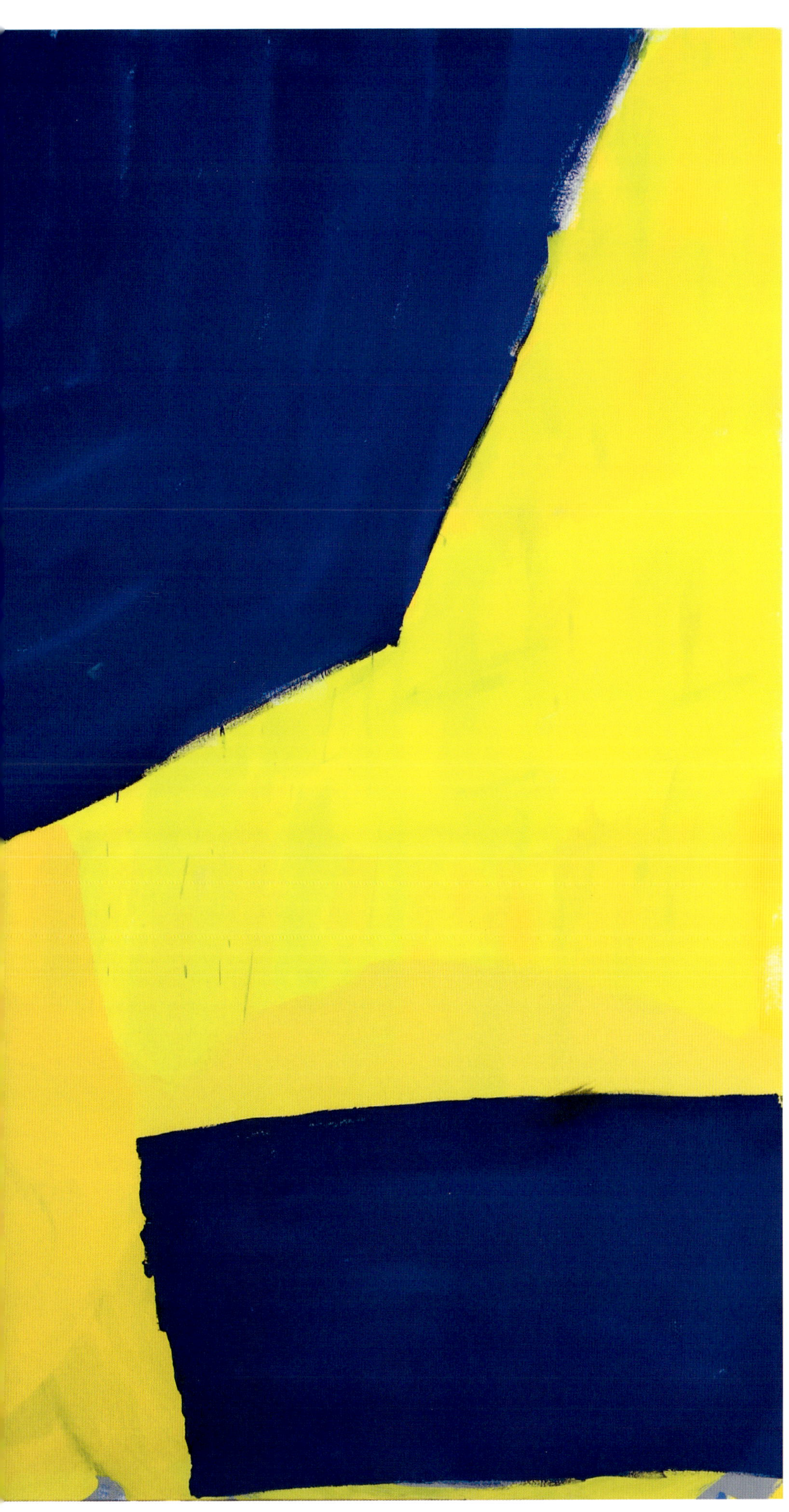

Siteplan Studio, 2009
Diptych
Acrylics | Pigment | Canvas
94.5 x 110.2 in. | 240 x 280 cm

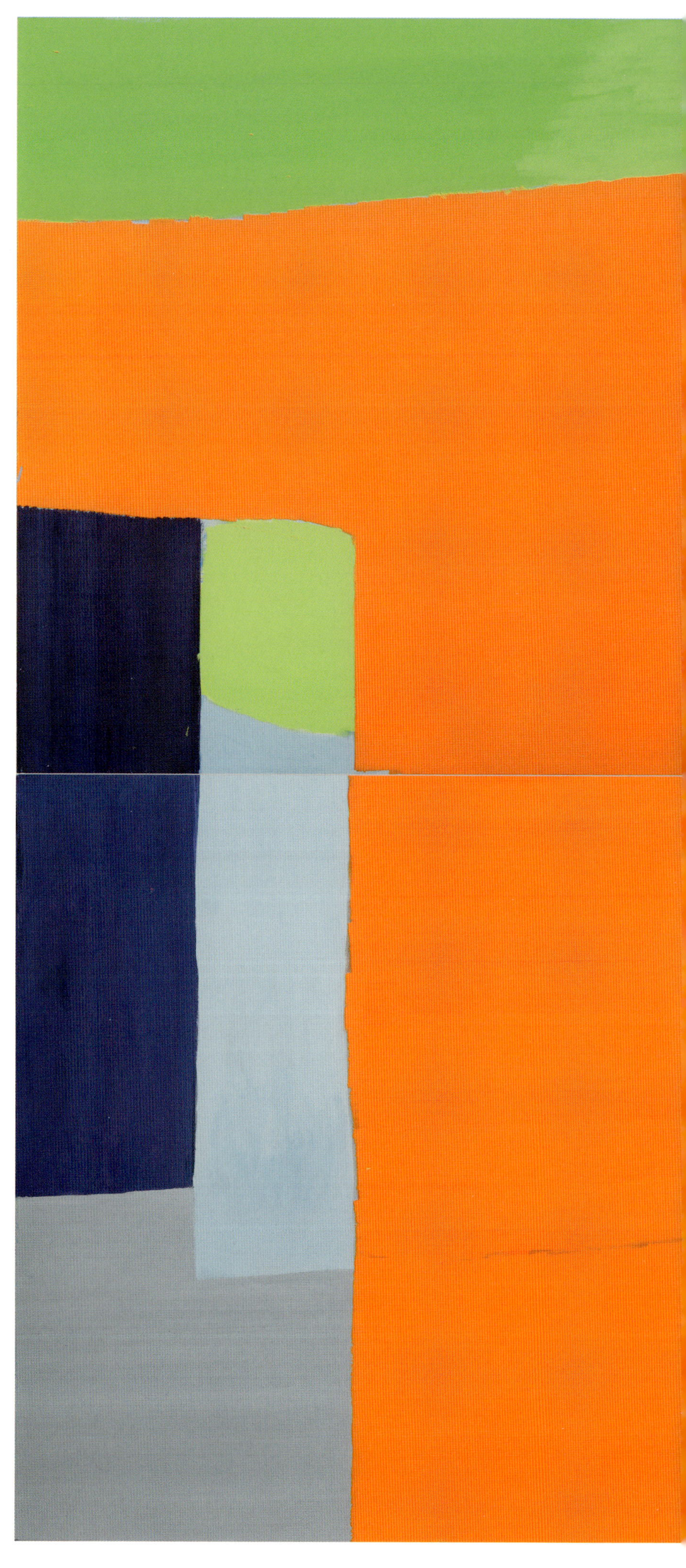

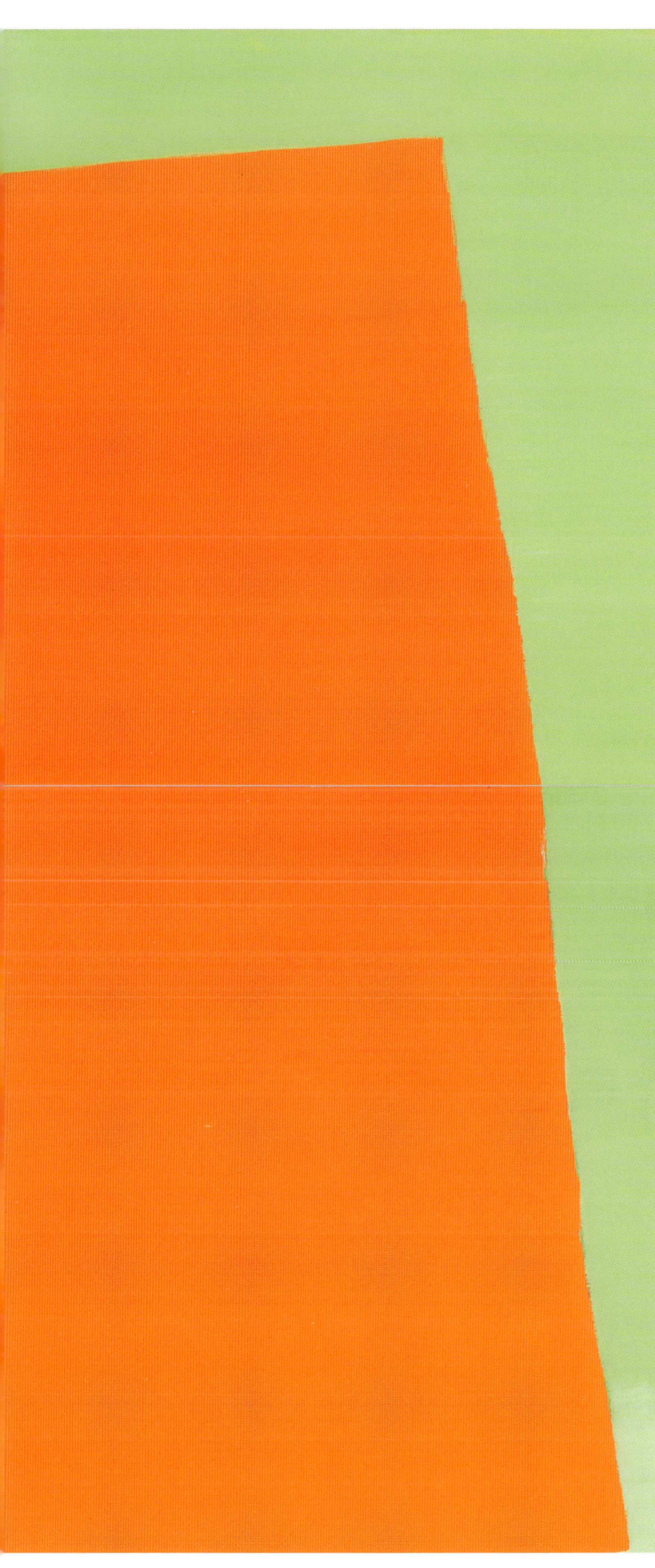

Siteplan Orange Place, 2013
Quadriptych
Egg tempera | Pigment | Canvas
78.7 x 78.7 in. | 200 x 200 cm

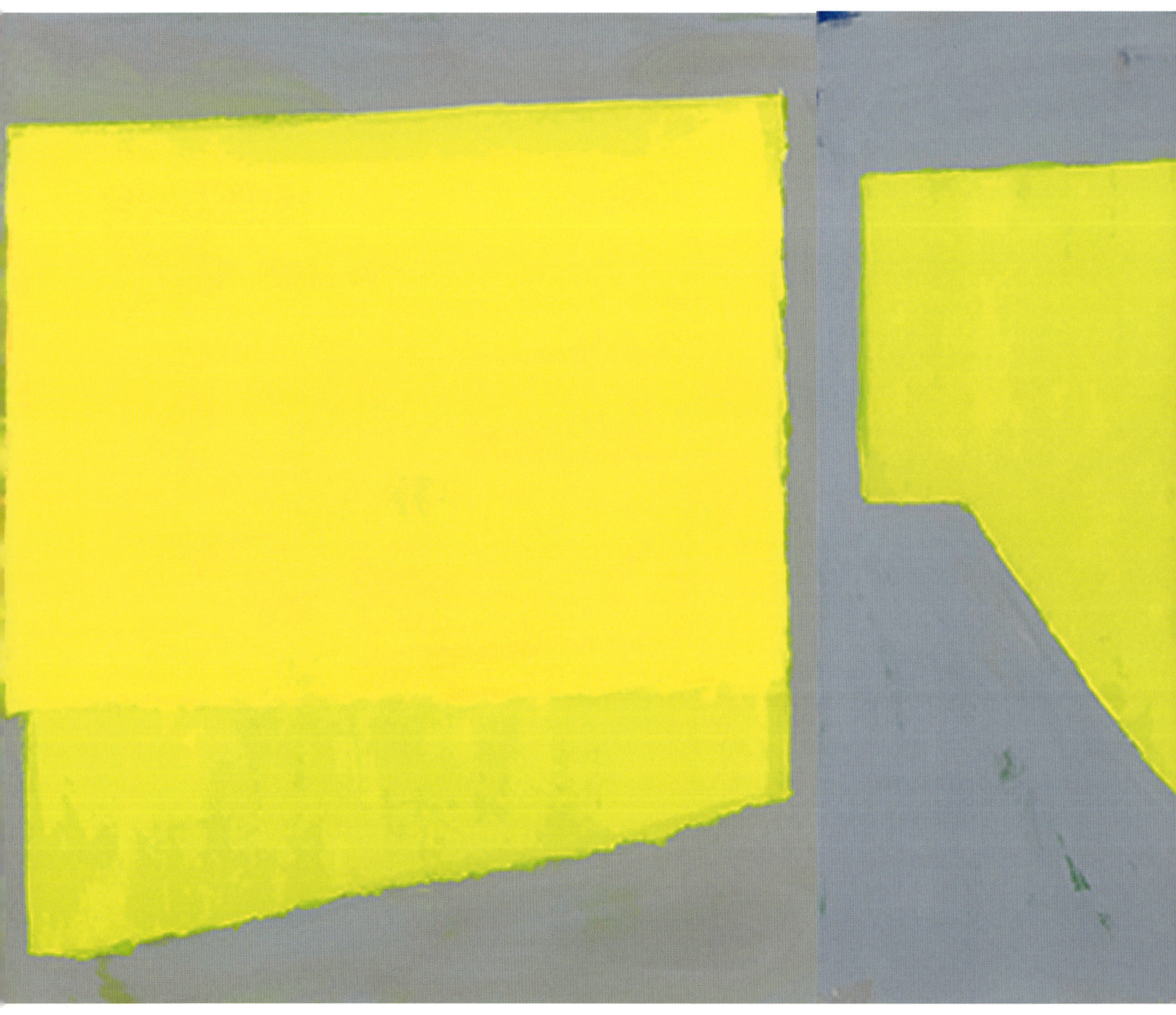

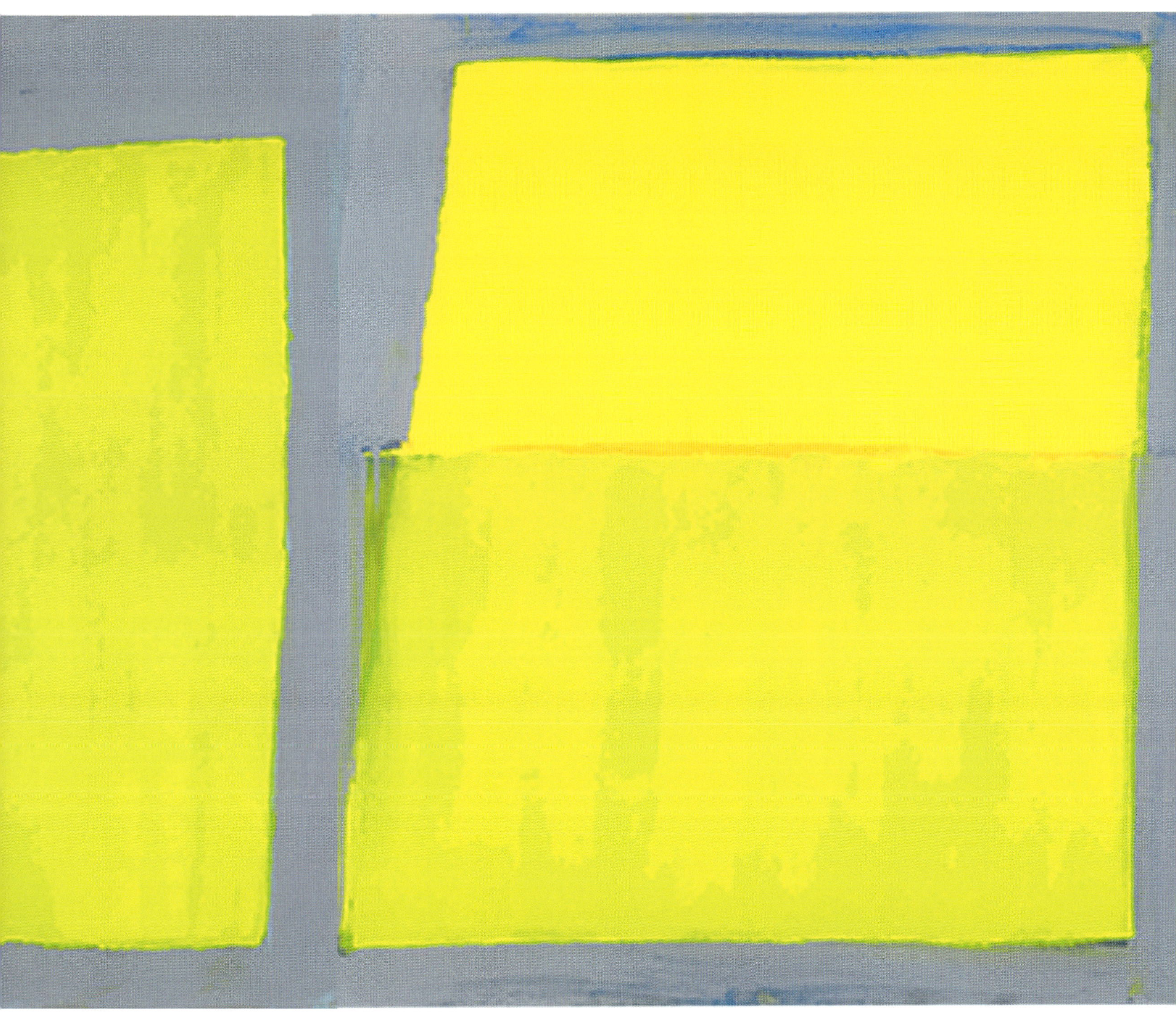

Siteplan Yellow Place, 2009
Triptych
Acrylics | Pigment | Canvas
55.1 x 141.3 in. | 140 x 360 cm

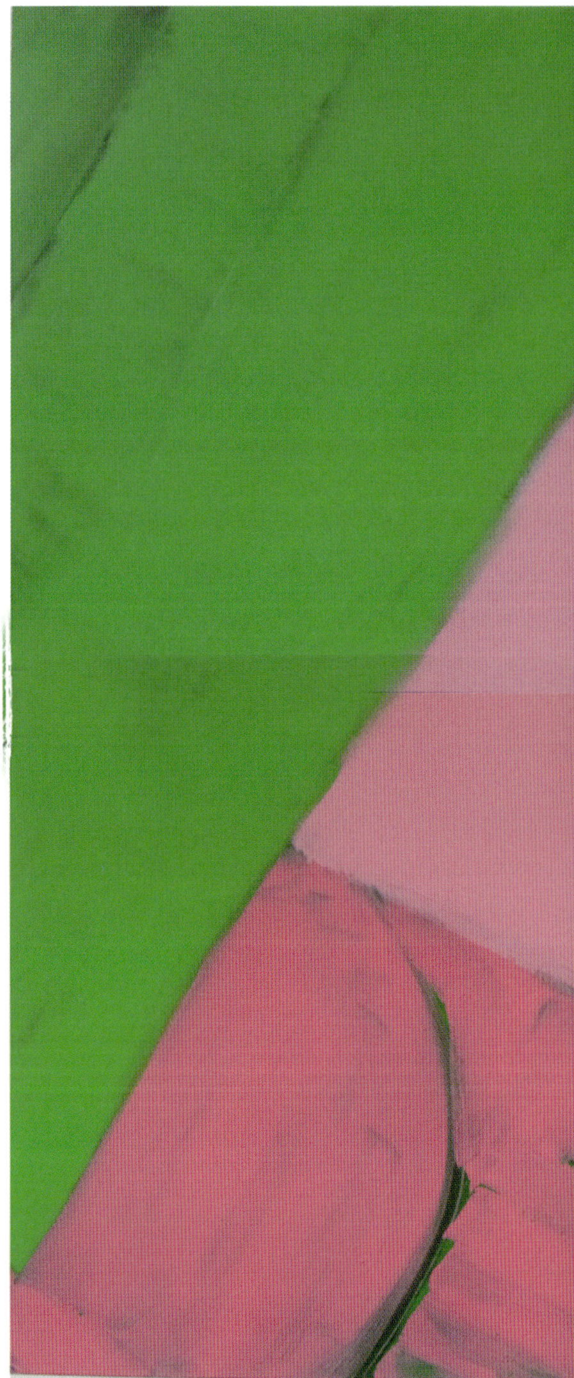

Sitemap Central Park, 2010
Septych
Acrylics | Pigment | Canvas
118,1 x 118.1 in. | 300 x 300 cm

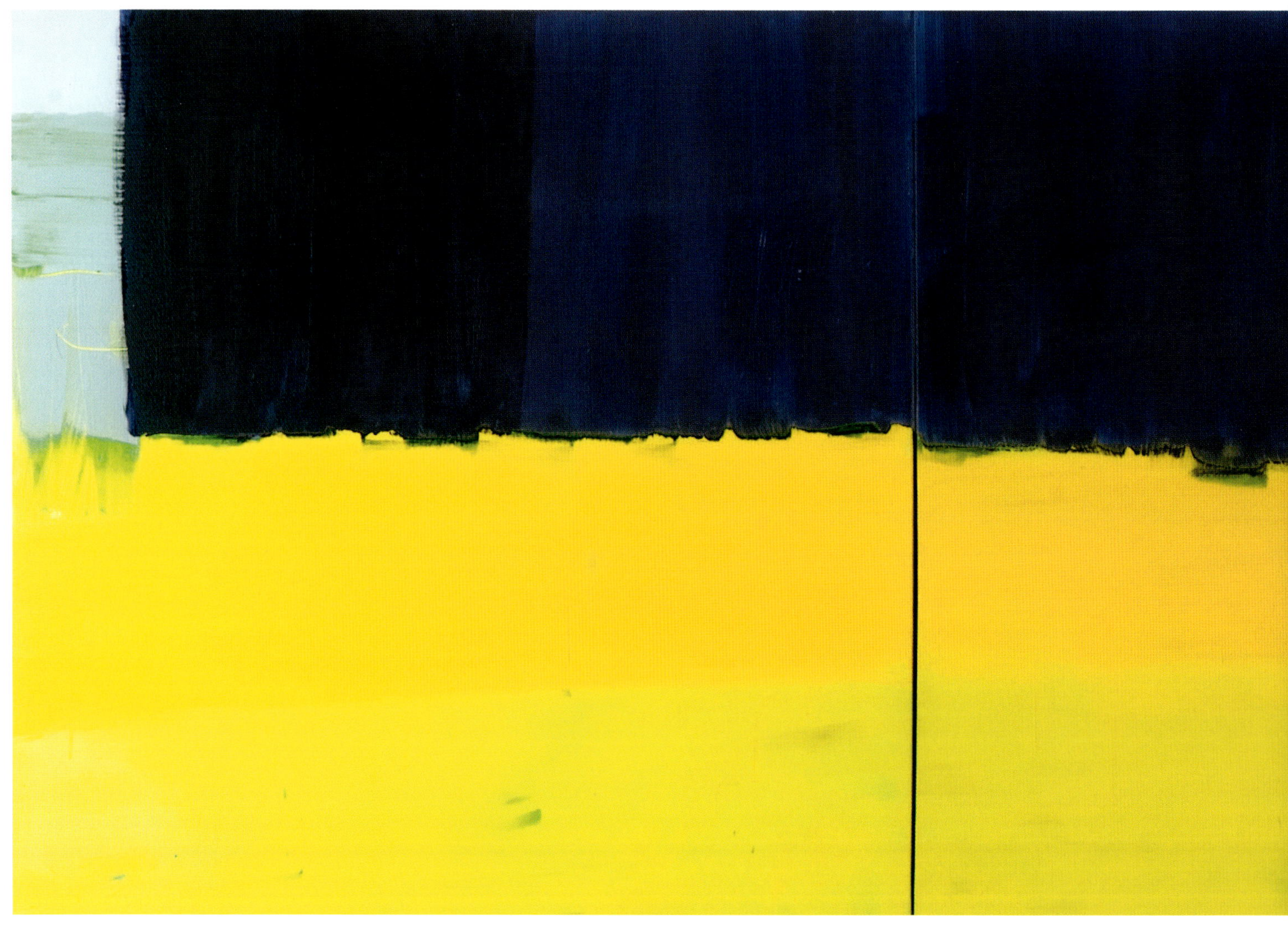

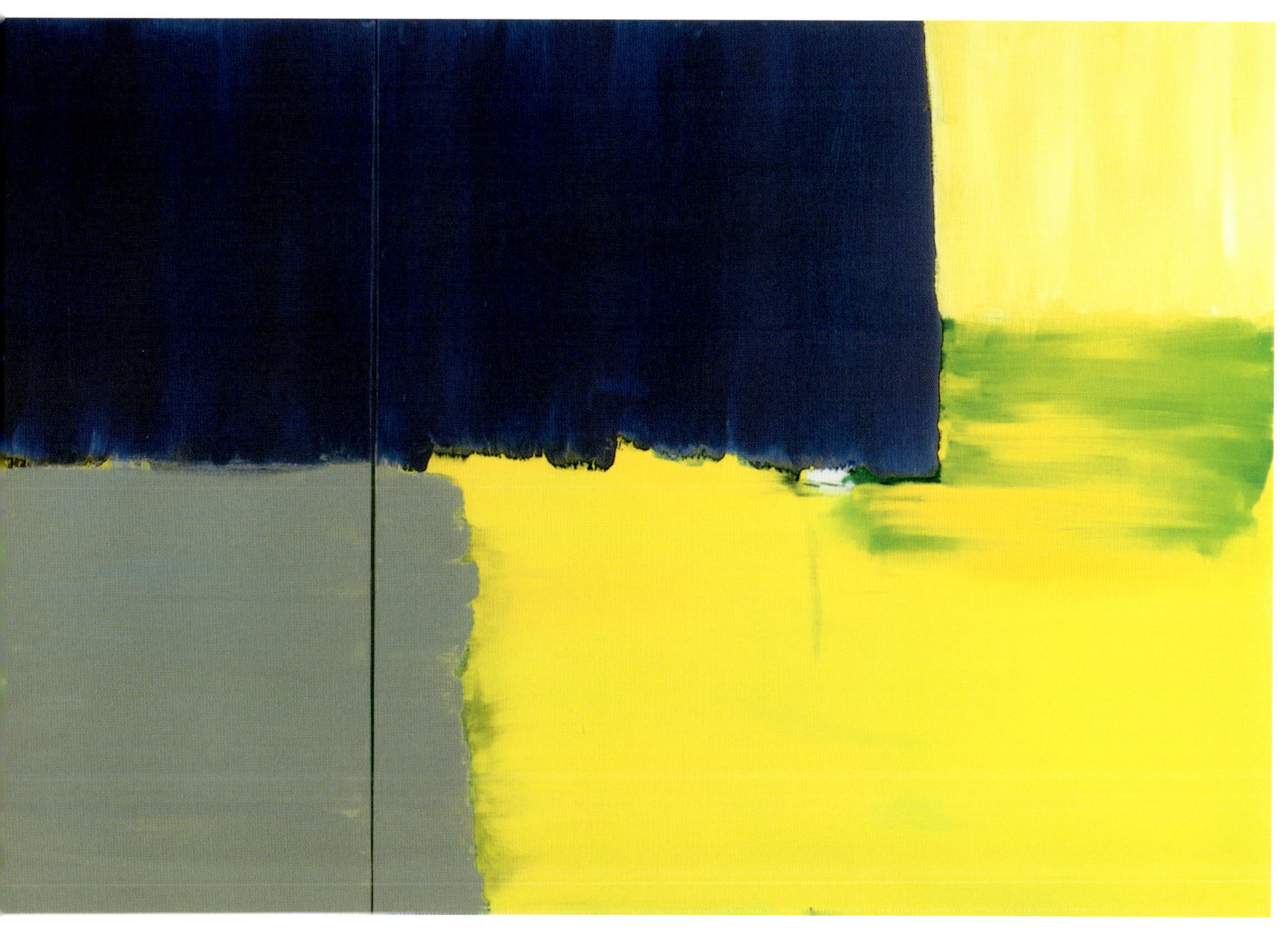

Siteplan Panorama, 2008
Triptych
Acrylics | Pigment | Canvas
39.4 x 118.1 in. | 100 x 300 cm
Public collection: Municipal Building Authority

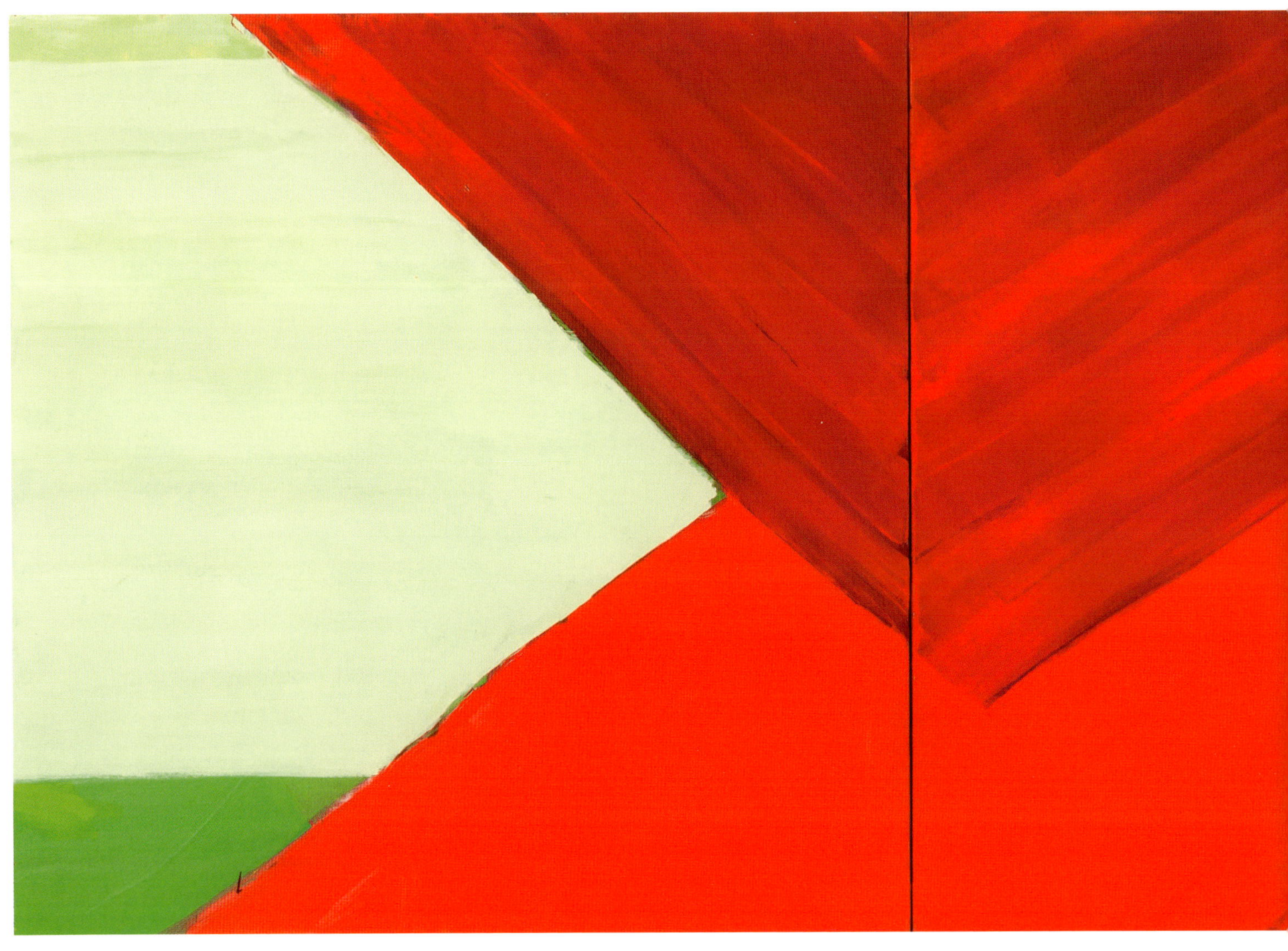

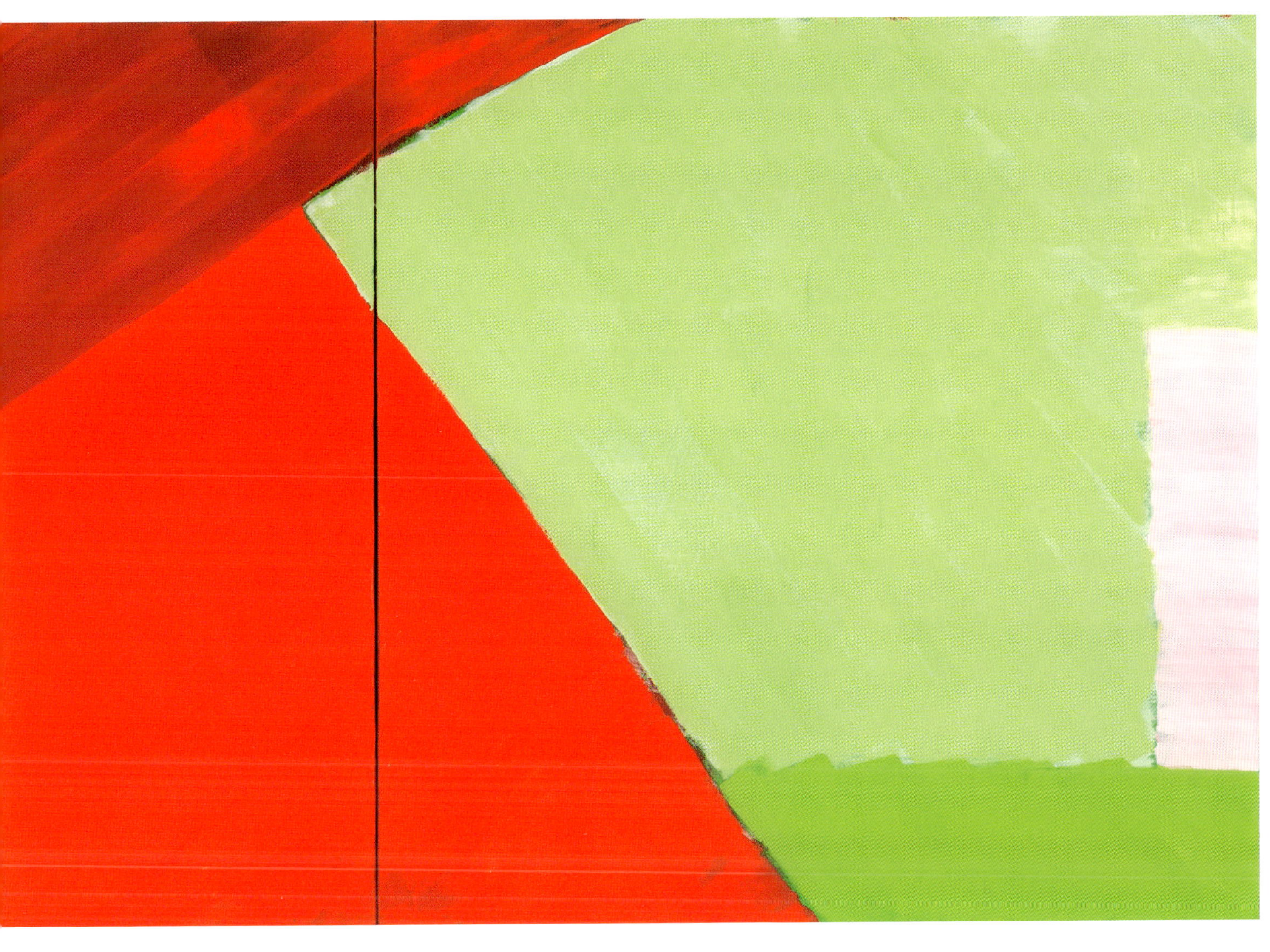

Siteplan Bulgaria, 2014
Triptych
Egg tempera | Pigment | Canvas
39.4 x 118.1 in. | 100 x 300 cm

# Lageplan

## Apokalypse | Offenbarung

# Siteplan

## Apocalypse / Revelation

Elvira Lantenhammer ist im weltbekannten Wallfahrtsort Altötting aufgewachsen und wurde in der Werkstatt eines Kirchenmalers zur Restauratorin ausgebildet. Religiöse Rituale und Bilder mit Engelsgestalten und Heiligenfiguren als Zeugen von Volksfrömmigkeit und spiritueller Suche sind allgegenwärtig. So ist es nicht überraschend, dass sie als Inspirationsquelle für ihren Zyklus „Lageplan Apokalypse/Offenbarung", der jüngst im Spitäle in Würzburg ausgestellt wurde, das biblische Thema der Offenbarung Johannis wählt und sich auf Albrecht Dürers Holzschnittfolge von 1498 bezieht. Bemerkenswert ist allerdings, wie stimmig es ihr gelingt, dieses motiv- und figurenreiche Meisterwerk in ihre eigene kraftvolle Bildsprache umzusetzen.

Elvira Lantenhammer grew up in the world-famous pilgrimage destination Altötting and was trained as a re-storer in a church painter's workshop. Religious rituals and pictures with angelic figures and statues of saints as witnesses of popular piety and spiritual search are omnipresent. So it is not surprising that she chooses the biblical theme of the Revelation of John as a source of inspiration for her cycle "Siteplan Apocalypse/Rev-elation," which was recently exhibited in the Spitäle in Würzburg, and refers to Albrecht Dürer's series of woodcuts from 1498. It is remarkable, however, how harmoniously she succeeds in translating this masterpiece rich in motifs and figures into her own powerful pictorial language.

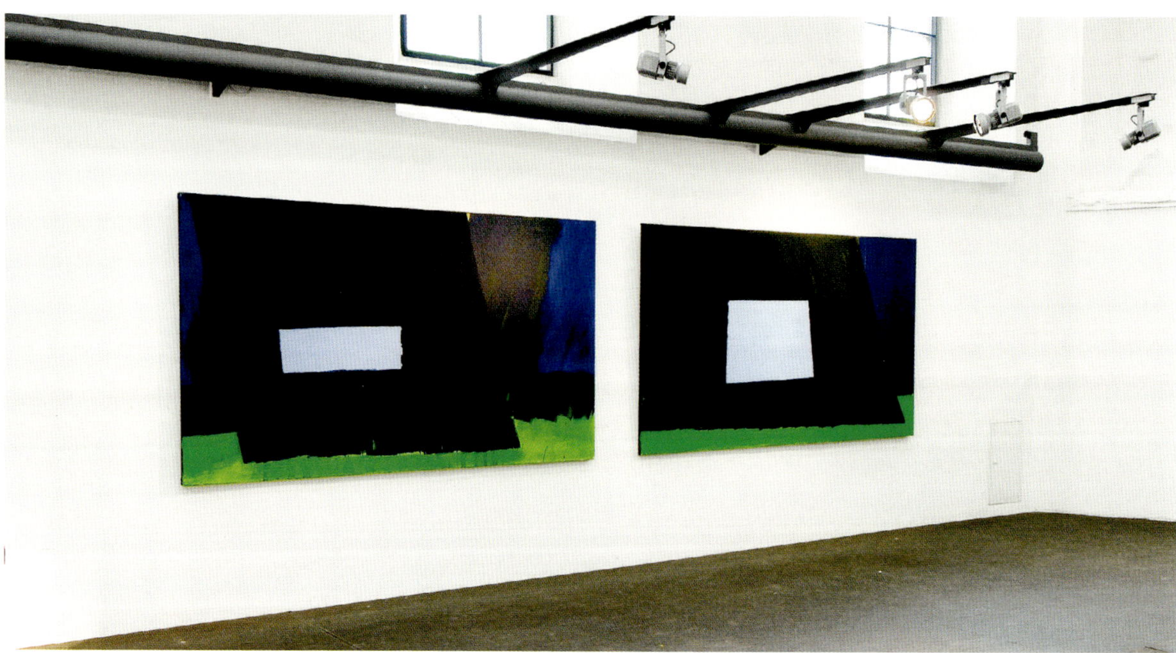

Apokalypse, 2017
Installation Spitäle Würzburg

Der siebenteilige Zyklus wird von einem tiefen, vitalen Schwarz zusammengehalten und in Bewegung gebracht. Es verdrängt zunehmend ein auf der ersten Leinwand noch dominantes, fast grelles Grün sowie ein leuchtendes Ultramarinblau und verdüstert die fünfte Leinwand fast vollständig. Erst auf den beiden letzten Bildern lichtet sich die Folge wieder und Grün und Blau kehren zurück; eine hellblaue Fläche erobert sich die Bildmitte vor dem schwarzen Vorhang.

Mitbestimmend an der starken Wirkung des Zyklus sind nicht nur Komposition und Farbwahl, sondern auch ein besonderes Augenmerk auf die Qualität der Farbmaterie. Um diese zu erreichen, mischt Elvira Lantenhammer die Farben selbst aus Acrylbindemittel und Pigmenten. Durch diese handwerkliche Arbeit können leichte Unregelmäßigkeiten wie Pigmentballungen oder Farbschlieren im Material verbleiben, die sich auch später in der Materie als belebendes Moment bemerkbar machen. Durch die veränderliche Konsistenz entstehen zudem unterschiedlich reflektierende Oberflächen. Die Farbfelder und besonders der schwarze Vorhang entstehen aus

The seven-part cycle is held together and set in motion by a deep, vital black. It increasingly replaces a dominant, almost garish green and a luminous ultramarine blue on the first canvas and darkens the fifth almost completely. Only in the last two pictures does the sequence lighten again, and green and blue return; a light blue surface occupies the middle of the picture in front of the black curtain.

The strong effect of the cycle is not only determined by the composition and choice of colors, but also by a special focus on the quality of the color matter. In order to achieve this, Elvira Lantenhammer mixes the colors herself from acrylic binders and pigments. This craftsmanship allows slight irregularities such as pigment clusters or streaks of color to remain in the material, which later become noticeable in the material as an invigorating moment. The variable consistency also creates surfaces with different reflections. The color fields and especially the black curtain are created by super-

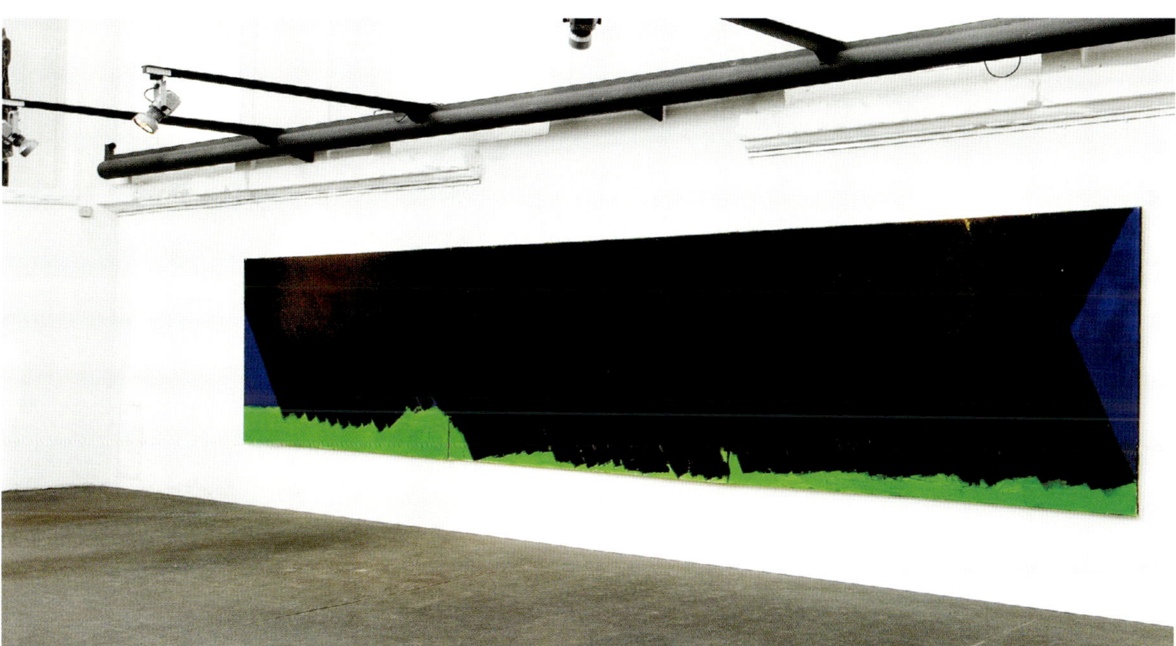

über- und nebeneinandergesetzten Pinselbahnen. In die breiten Pinselstriche legt die Künstlerin die in ihrem ganzen Körper erspürte Bewegung, die sich so unvermittelt auf die Leinwand überträgt. Die ausladende Geste bestimmt das Format des Bildes mit.

Elvira Lantenhammer arbeitet abstrakt. Auch wenn es in die Farbmaterie eingekratzte grafische Elemente gibt, die auf Konstruktionen oder Räume hinweisen könnten, bleibt sie immer gegenstandslos. Gerade bei Werken, die sich auf einen erzählerischen Text und figürliche Darstellungen beziehen, kommt die Frage auf, inwieweit ungegenständliche Kunst narrativ bzw. symbolisch sein kann. Die Folge „Lageplan Apokalypse/Offenbarung", die sowohl zyklisch als auch linear gelesen werden kann, bejaht diese Frage, auch wenn die Bedeutung der symbolistisch agierenden Momente nicht vollständig dechiffriert werden. Die Symbolik ist modern offen und nicht wie in Dürers Holzstichfolge von strengen ikonografischen Vorgaben festgelegt. Albrecht Dürer arbeitet in seinen Szenen grundsätzlich am Bibeltext. In seinen Holzstichen greift er auf Bildlösungen der abendländischen Tradition zurück und reichert sie mit eigenen Skizzen und Bildideen an. Waren damals allegorische Figuren wie die vier Apokalyptischen Reiter oder die Frau mit dem Drachen noch geläufig, kennt man sie heute wohl nur noch im bibelaffinen Umfeld. Der Text zielt auf ein Erlösungsversprechen und auf Belohnung für alle Frommen, die Gott verehren. Im Bewusstsein bleiben jedoch eher schreckliche Plagen und Strafen wie Feuer, Kometen und tödliche Krankheiten, mit denen Sünder und Abweichler bestraft werden. Selbst heute ist „Apokalypse" immer noch ein Synonym für Strafgericht und Weltuntergang. Und genau dieses thematisiert Elvira Lantenhammer in ihrem Bildzyklus.

Mit der ungegenständlichen Malweise folgt sie stringent einem Weg, den sie schon seit Jahren mit ihren Lageplänen

imposed and juxtaposed brush strokes. The artist brings the movement felt in her whole body into the broad brush strokes, which is thus immediately transferred to the canvas. The sweeping gesture also determines the format of the picture.

Elvira Lantenhammer works abstractly. Even if there are graphic elements scratched into the color matter that could point to constructions or spaces, it always remains abstract. Especially in works that refer to narrative text and figurative representations, the question arises to what extent non-objective art can be narrative or symbolic. The sequence "Siteplan Apocalypse/Revelation," which can be read both cyclically and linearly, affirms this question, even if the meaning of the symbolically acting moments is not completely deciphered. The symbolism is modernly open and not, as in Dürer's sequence of wood engravings, determined by strict iconographic specifications. Albrecht Dürer basically works on the Bible text in his scenes. In his wood engravings he draws on pictorial solutions from the occidental tradition and enriches them with his own sketches and pictorial ideas. While allegorical figures such as the four apocalyptic horsemen or the woman with the dragon were still familiar at the time, today they are probably only known in biblical environments. The text aims at a promise of salvation and a reward for all pious people who worship God. However, the consciousness remains rather of terrible plagues and punishments such as fire, comets and deadly diseases, with which sinners and dissenters are punished. Even today, the term "apocalypse" is still synonymous with punishment and the end of the world. And this is exactly what Elvira Lantenhammer thematizes in her pictorial cycle.

With her non-representational style of painting she stringently follows a path that she has been following

geht. Die auf Städte in Deutschland und Übersee verweisenden Lagepläne entstehen seit 1996. Es sind Flächenbilder, die ihre Wirkung aus sparsamen, aber kraftvollen Farbkombinationen und klaren Kompositionen erhalten. Die Künstlerin betont, dass es sich nicht um Stadtpläne oder Karten mit topografischen Besonderheiten handelt, sondern um die Aufzeichnung dessen, was sie emotional, haptisch oder sensorisch mit einem Ort verbindet. So erscheint der Lageplan Rom in einem kräftigen Rot, der sich kaum aus dem täglich erlebbaren Stadtbild oder einem Stadtplan erklären lässt, jedoch mit Seheindrücken vor Ort, die von Gemälden, Gewändern oder anderen Gegenständen kommen könnten, mit denen sie sich gerade beschäftigte. Es sind innere Landkarten, die vom titelgebenden Ort ausgehen, sich aber dann von ihm lösen.

Wie der „Lageplan Atlantis" bezieht sich auch der „Lageplan Apokalypse/Offenbarung" auf etwas Legendäres, in diesem Fall auf eine biblische Vision. Wie in den Lageplänen nimmt sie einen für sie wichtigen Punkt heraus und setzt ihn schlüssig um. Vorher hatte sie jedoch äußerst selten Schwarz verwendet, nun nutzt sie es, um den Weltuntergang auszudrücken. Wird das Schwarz in dem ersten Bild als trennende Setzung zwischen blauen und grünen Farbflächen benutzt, nimmt es in Folge dramatisch zu und verdeckt immer mehr die farbigen Flächen. Das fast gänzlich schwarze Bild zeugt vom vollzogenen Weltuntergang, der allerdings nicht zwangsläufig das Ende bedeutet.

In Dürers Holzschnitten hingegen verschwärzt sich die Szenerie deutlich weniger, sowohl zeichnerisch als auch inhaltlich. Auch wenn Erzfeinde auftreten und Widersacher geschlagen werden, ist immer das Heil als Symbol oder Figur im Bild gegenwärtig. Nach der Apokalypse werden die Frommen ohne Leid sein und ihren Lohn erhalten und regieren; das Himmlische Jerusalem erscheint im Bild.

for years with her siteplans. The siteplans, which refer to cities in Germany and overseas, are being created since 1996. They are area paintings that get their effect from economical but powerful color combinations and clear compositions. The artist emphasizes that these are not city maps or maps with topographical peculiarities, but rather recordings of what she associates emotionally, haptically, or sensory with a place. Thus the siteplan of Rome appears in a strong red, which can hardly be explained by the daily experience of the cityscape or a city map, but with visual impressions on the spot, which could come from paintings, robes or other objects that she was currently occupied with. These are inner maps that emanate from the place that gave the title, but then detach themselves from it.

Like the "Siteplan Atlantis," the "Siteplan Apocalypse/Revelation" refers to something legendary, in this case a biblical vision. As in the siteplans, it takes out an important point for them and implements it conclusively. Before, however, she rarely used black, but now she uses it to express the end of the world. If black is used in the first picture as a separating set between blue and green colored areas, it increases dramatically and covers more and more the colored areas. The almost entirely black picture bears witness to the end of the world, which, however, does not necessarily mean the end.

In Dürer's woodcuts, on the other hand, the scenery becomes much less black, both in terms of drawing and content. Even when arch-enemies appear and adversaries are beaten, salvation is always present in the picture as a symbol or figure. After the Apocalypse, the pious will be without suffering and will receive and reign their reward; the Heavenly Jerusalem appears in the picture.

Zerstörung und Erlösung kann man auch in Elvira Lantenhammers Zyklus finden: Nach dem alles verschluckenden Schwarz hellen sich die beiden letzten Bilder wieder auf. Blau und Grün bekommen wieder mehr Raum und ein Hellblau kommt in der Bildmitte hinzu. Ist es zu kühn, die angebotene Farbsymbolik ernst zu nehmen, und Blau und Grün für Hoffnung und Leben zu nehmen, das Schwarz für den strafenden Zorn Gottes und Leid und das hellblaue Quadrat als paradiesisches Himmlisches Jerusalem? Ganz abwegig ist der Gedanke nicht, jedoch liegt der Künstlerin solch eine semantisch vereinfachende Auslegung fern, ebenso wie eine lineare Lesart.

Sie begreift die sieben Bilder als einen Zyklus: Nun könnte, allerdings mit verändertem Ausgangspunkt, der Zyklus von Vergehen und neuem Werden wieder beginnen, eine Möglichkeit, die in Dürers Erzählung nicht gegeben ist, die mit der Vision eines Heilsversprechens endet. Das Veränderliche, die Vorstellung des Lebens in Zyklen, ist weniger im westlichen als im asiatischen Denken verhaftet, das sich Elvira Lantenhammer durch die Praxis der Zen-Meditation zu eigen gemacht hat. Der Zyklus erscheint weniger als das Strafgericht eines ungnädigen Gottes denn als eine innere Vision der Künstlerin selbst, die sich mit Leben und Sterben auseinandersetzt. Das Dunkle wird nicht pathetisiert. Es ist monumental, verliert allerdings durch das Zurückweichen seinen Schrecken. Nach Zeiten des Leidens kommt die Zeit des hoffungsfrohen Weiterentwickelns, allerdings von einem veränderten Ausgangspunkt aus, denn es ist nicht mehr möglich, an den Ort des Ursprungs zurückzukommen. Das Leben ist ein Kreislauf, in dem vieles wiederkehrt, wenn auch verändert – eine je nach Standpunkt tröstliche oder beunruhigende Vorstellung. Die Perspektive der Künstlerin ist vorwärts gewandt: Sie zeigt uns eine hoffnungsfrohe Vision voller lebendiger Farbe ohne Ängstlichkeit, die sich vor einem gegenwärtigen Schwarz behauptet. Das Vergehen wird ein Nicht-Vergehen.

Hanneke Heinemann

Destruction and redemption can also be found in Elvira Lantenhammer's cycle: after the swallowing black, the last two images brighten up again. Blue and green get more space again and a light blue is added in the middle of the picture. Is it too bold to take the offered color symbolism seriously and to take blue and green for hope and life, the black for the punishing wrath of God and suffering and the light blue square as paradi-siac Heavenly Jerusalem? The idea is not entirely absurd, but such a semantically simplistic interpretation is far removed from the artist, as is a linear reading.

She understands the seven pictures as a cycle: now, albeit with a changed starting point, the cycle of passing away and new creation could begin again, a possibility that is not given in Dürer's narrative, which ends with the vision of a promise of salvation. The changeable, the idea of life in cycles, is less rooted in Western than in Asian thinking, which Elvira Lantenhammer has made her own through the practice of Zen meditation. The cycle appears less as the punishment of an ungracious God than as an inner vision of the artist herself who deals with life and death. The dark is not infused with pathos. It is monumental, but loses its horror by retreating. After times of suffering, the time of hopeful further development comes, however from a changed starting point, because it is no longer possible to return to the place of origin. Life is a cycle in which much returns, albeit changed, depending on one's point of view, a comforting or disturbing notion. The artist's perspective is forward looking: she shows us a hopeful vision full of vivid color without anxiety, which asserts itself in front of a contemporary black. The passing away becomes a non-passing away.

Hanneke Heinemann

## Apokalypse

## Apocalypse

Vielfalt
Von Schwarz überrollt werden
Ganz und gar im Schwarz sein
Aus dem Schwarz / aus dem Nichts
entsteht das Neue

diversity
overrun by black
being completely in the black
from the black / from nothing
the new emerges

Siteplan Apocalypse, 2011
Acrylics | Pigment | Canvas
11.8 x 47.2 in. | 30 x 120 cm

NEXT PAGE:
Apocalypse, 2010
Acrylics | Pigment | Canvas
55.1 x 78.7 in. | 140 x 200 cm

Apocalypse, 2010
Triptych
Acrylics | Pigment | Canvas
each 55,1 x 78,7 in. | 140 x 200 cm

NEXT PAGE:
Apocalypse, 2010
Acrylics | Pigment | Canvas
55,1 x 78,7 in. | 140 x 200 cm

Apocalypse, 2010
Acrylics | Pigment | Canvas
55,1 x 78,7 in. | 140 x 200 cm

Apocalypse, 2010
Acrylics | Pigment | Canvas
55,1 x 78,7 in. | 140 x 200 cm

# Kakemono
## Japanese Siteplan

Die „Arbeit Kakemono - Japanese Siteplan", aus Japan mitgebracht, war für mich überraschender als erwartet. Nicht nur wegen des Formates mit einer Länge von zwölf Metern, sondern wegen der Wirkung der verwendeten tagesleuchtenden, farbsatten Neonfarben. Sie treten nun kraftvoll mit einer gelassenen Selbstverständlichkeit in ihre neuen Werke hinein. Die Reise und die Begegnung mit dem Sehnsuchtsland Japan haben unübersehbar neue Energien freigesetzt.

Zwar wiesen ihre Lagepläne schon früher eine signalhafte Farbigkeit auf, die Künstlerin hatte auch schon immer den Mut, auch Komplementärkontraste gegeneinanderzustellen. Doch schien sie am Anfang noch etwas zu zögern, schien ihrer Intuition nicht ganz trauen zu wollen, denn sie sieht in den ersten Studien zunächst noch nicht durchgängig das un-

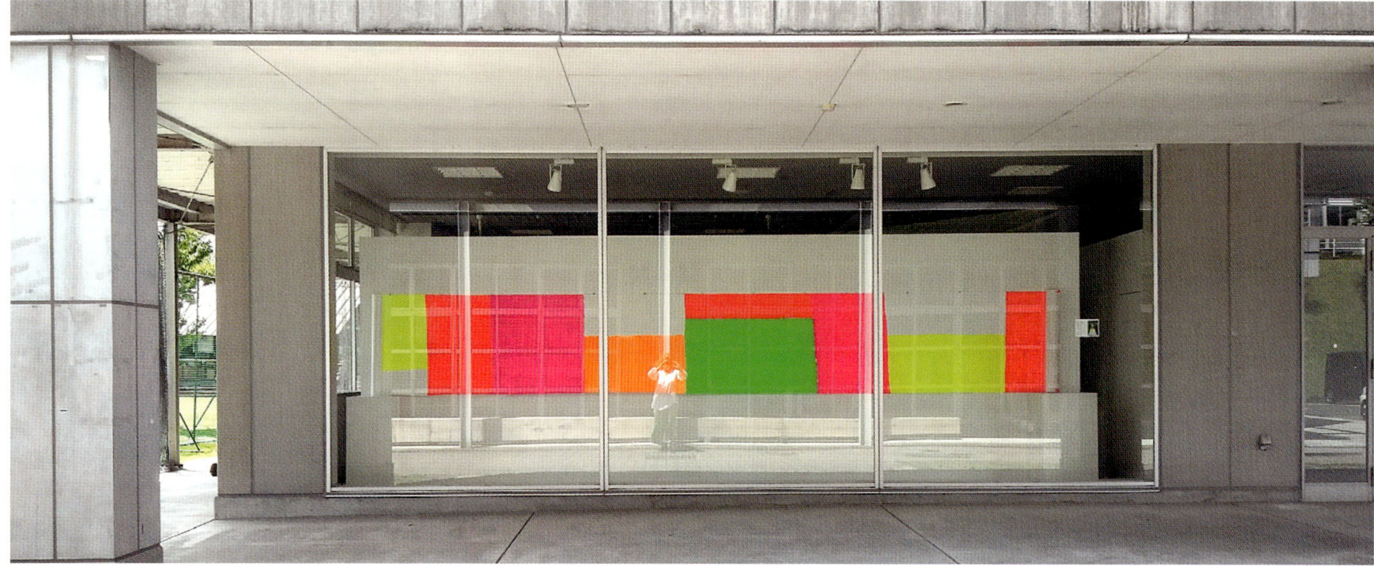

Kakemono - Japanese Siteplan
Windows Gallery, Otus, Japan 2017

# Kakemono
## Japanese Siteplan

The work "Kakemono – Japanese Siteplan," brought from Japan, was for me more surprising than expected. Not only because of the format with a length of twelve meters, but also because of the effect of the day-lit, colorful neon colors used. They now powerfully enter her new works with a relaxed naturalness. The journey and the encounter with Japan, the land of longing, have clearly released new energies.

Although her site plans had already shown a signal-like coloration in the past, the artist has always had the courage to contrast complementary contrasts with each other. But at the beginning she seemed to hesitate a little, she didn't seem to trust her intuition completely, because in the first studies she initially didn't foresee

mittelbare Aufeinanderstoßen der Farben vor. Sie setzt noch schwarze Felder dazwischen. Das Schwarz benutzt sie gerne als Trennung zwischen Farben und als Akzentsetzung. Hier tritt im Laufe der Entwicklung des Kakemono nun eine Änderung ein: Die direkte, geballte Verwendung der leuchtenden Farben im Rollbild ist unübersehbar eine neue Qualität.

Unter welchen Bedingungen ist denn nun „Kakemono – Japanese Siteplan" entstanden?

Elvira Lantenhammers letztjähriger Aufenthalt in Japan bestand aus zwei Etappen. Zunächst wohnte und arbeitete sie in Itoshima in der Provinz Fukuoka auf der südlichen Hauptinsel in Japan. Das dortige Studio Kura bietet in mehreren Häusern Künstlern aus aller Welt Platz zur Arbeit und zum Austausch. Auf der Holzterrasse eines nahe gelegenen Schreins macht sie ihre Tai-Chi-Übungen, von hier aus unternimmt sie Fahrradtouren durch die Reisfelder und ans Meer. Sie spürt die Hitze und Feuchtigkeit in der Luft, genießt die Blicke auf die freie See und saugt die Natur in sich auf. Hier entstehen einige kleinere Arbeiten und die ersten sieben Meter des Kakemono. Der Aufenthalt in der ländlichen Region und der Austausch mit Künstlerkolleginnen und -kollegen tragen sehr zu den wesentlichen künstlerischen Findungen bei. Dann reist sie in Würzburgs Partnerstadt Otsu auf der Hauptinsel, wo sie an dem erstmals stattfindenden Künstleraustausch der beiden Städte teilnehmen darf. Sie bekommt eine Wohnung und eine Atelierplatz gestellt und erhält eine Ausstellungsmöglichkeit an der Seian University of Art and Design in Otsu. Hinter der langen Fensterfront der Windows Gallery auf dem Campus kann sie viele Meter des Kakemono ausstellen. Durch die Nähe

the immediate colliding of the colors. She still places black fields between them. She likes to use black as a separation between colors and as an accent. In the course of developing the Kakemono, a change occurs: the direct, concentrated use of the bright colors in the scroll picture is a new quality that cannot be overlooked.

Under what conditions was the "Kakemono – Japanese Siteplan" created?

Elvira Lantenhammer's stay in Japan last year consisted of two stages. First she lived and worked in Itoshima in the province Fukuoka on the southern main island in Japan. The Studio Kura there offers artists from all over the world space for work and exchange in several houses. She does her Tai Chi exercises on the wooden terrace of a nearby shrine, from where she undertakes bicycle tours through the rice fields and to the sea. She feels the heat and humidity in the air, enjoys the views of the sea, and absorbs nature. Some smaller works and the first seven meters of the Kakemono are created here. The stay in the rural region and the exchange with fellow artists contribute greatly to the essential artistic discoveries. Then she travels to Würzburg's twin city Otsu on the main island, where she is allowed to take part in the artists' exchange between the two cities, which is taking place for the first time. She will be given an apartment and a studio space and will have the opportunity to exhibit at the Seian University of Art and Design in Otsu. Behind the long window front of the Windows Gallery on campus, she can exhibit

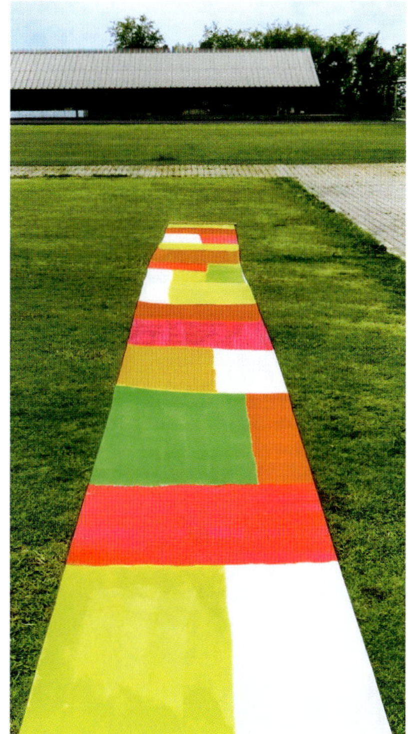

Kakemono - Japanese Siteplan
Campus Seian University for Arts and Design
Otus, Japan 2017

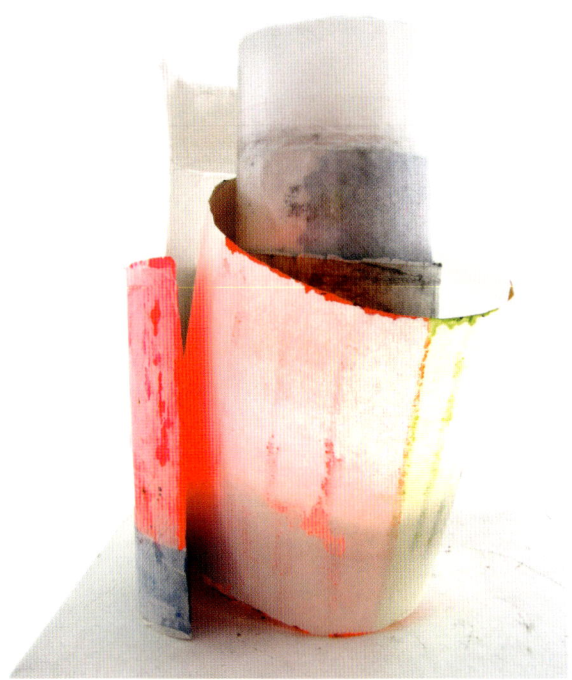

Japanese Siteplan
Kakemono, rolled up

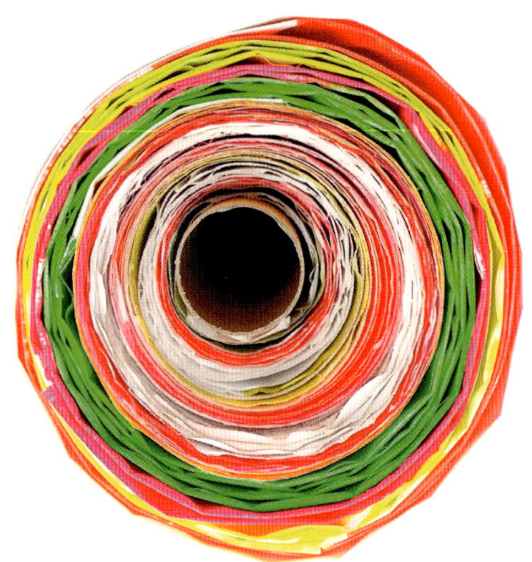

zu Kyoto und vielen wichtigen Stätten und Monumenten erfüllt sich ein langgehegter Traum für sie und sie kann Orte, die ihr lange nur durch Abbildungen bekannt waren, nun selbst persönlich besuchen. Während eines ihrer siebzehn Ausflüge nach Kyoto weilt und meditiert sie beispielsweise im berühmten Ryōan-ji-Zen-Garten („Tempel des zur Ruhe gekommenen Drachens").

Es gehört zum Konzept von Elvira Lantenhammer, dass sie immer mit Materialien arbeitet, die sie sich vor Ort besorgt. Mit den neuen Farben und Untergründen fällt es ihr noch leichter, sich dem Ort anzunähern.

Das Papier hat sich Elvira Lantenhammer in einem ortsansässigen Baumarkt besorgt. Es ist besonders reißfest und wird für Shōjis, also typische japanische Raumteiler verwendet, in denen das halbtransparente Papier zwischen Holzrahmen gespannt wird. Bevor sie die richtige Auswahl trifft, hat sie mehrere Sorten auf Klebeverhalten und Bemalbarkeit geprüft. Die Farben hat sie auch in Japan selbst hergestellt, die Pigmente fand sie in einem üppig ausgestatteten Pigmentladen in Itoshima. Für „Kakemono – Japanese Siteplan" hat sie fluoreszierende Pigmente gewählt, die eine intensive Wirkung zeigen. Da sie die Pigmente selbst mischt, kann sie

many meters of Kakemono. Her proximity to Kyoto and many important sites and monuments makes a long-cherished dream come true for her and she can now personally visit places she has known for a long time only through illustrations. On one of her seventeen trips to Kyoto, for example, she stays and meditates in the famous Ryōan-ji-Zen-garden ("The Temple of the Drag-on at Peace").

It is part of Elvira Lantenhammer's concept that she always works with materials that she procures locally. With the new colors and backgrounds it is even easier for her to get closer to the place.

Elvira Lantenhammer obtained the paper from a local do-it-yourself store. It is particularly tear-resistant and is used for shōji, typical Japanese room dividers in which the semi-transparent paper is stretched between wooden frames. Before she makes the right choice, she has tested several types for adhesive properties and paint-ability. She also produced the paints herself in Japan, and found the pigments in a lavishly equipped pigment shop in Itoshima. For "Kakemono – Japanese Siteplan," she chose fluorescent pigments that have an intense

Deckung und Lasur in ihrem Sinne immer beeinflussen. So erweisen sie sich als absolut brauchbar für ihr künstlerisches Arbeiten.
Es existieren zwar mehrere Ideenskizzen zum Rollbild, das Kakemono selbst ist jedoch ohne Vorzeichnung entstanden und entwickelt sich letztendlich aus den schon vollendeten Partien. Das Tagwerk beginnt mit dem Ankleben eines neuen Stückes, auf dem sich aus den Farben, der Aufteilung und dem Auftrag des schon vorhandenen Bildes der neue Abschnitt entwickelt. Ab einem gewissen Arbeitsstand hat auch die Künstlerin kaum noch mehr die Möglichkeit, das gesamte Band auf einem Blick zu sehen. So ist dieser Prozess besonders offen für spontane Ideen und fängt auch die Tagesverfassung im besonderen Maß ein.

Die Farbflächen gestaltet Elvira Lantenhammer sehr differenziert und ausdrucksstark, vom dichten Auftrag mit vollem Pinsel bis zu zarten Lasierungen, die sich fast aufzulösen scheinen. Stellen, an denen das Papier durchscheint, wirken wie helle Bänder und Durchbrüche. Im ausführenden Gestus des Pinsels ist immer zu spüren, dass die Künstlerin nicht nur aus der Hand malt, sondern mit ihrem ganzen Körper. Viele Pinselstriche erfolgen im Atemrhythmus, was sich auch im Farbauftrag spüren lässt. Sie sind parallel wie die Striche eines Rechens, jedoch gerade gezogen. Sie müssen nicht wie

effect. Since she mixes the pigments herself, she can always influence coverage and glaze to her purport. Thus they prove to be absolutely useful for her artistic work.

Although there are several sketches of ideas for the scroll painting, the Kakemono itself was created without a preliminary drawing and ultimately develops from the finished parts. The day's work begins with the gluing of a new piece, on which the new section develops from the colors, the division and the application of the already existing picture. From a certain stage onwards, the artist hardly has the opportunity to see the entire scroll at once. Thus, this process is particularly open to spontaneous ideas and captures her own daily shape in a special way.

Elvira Lantenhammer creates the color surfaces in a very differentiated and expressive way, from dense application with a full brush to delicate glazes that almost seem to dissolve. Places where the paper shines through seem like light bands and breakthroughs. In the gesture of the brush, one can always feel that the artist does not only paint from her hand, but with her whole body. Many brush strokes take place in the rhythm of breathing, which can also be felt in the application of paint.

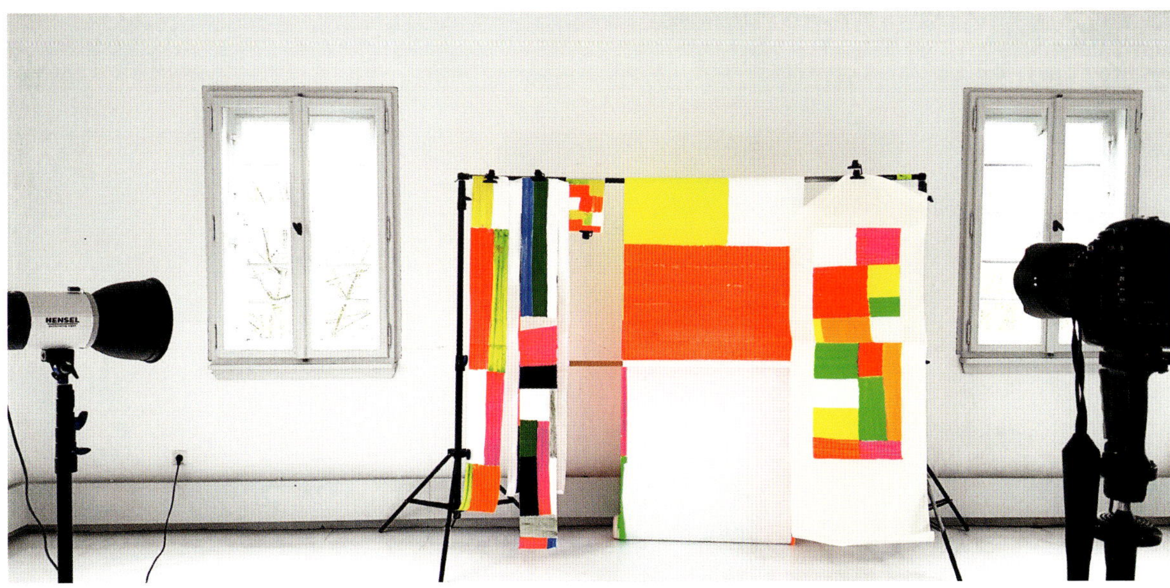


Kakemono - Japanese Siteplan
Installation Studio Schloss Homburg
2017

in ihren früheren Bildern von Zen-Gärten auf Steinsetzungen reagieren.

Auf dem Rollbild bleibt Platz für kleinere Imperfektionen und Naturähnliches: Leichte Auffaltungen im Papier bringen Spuren vom Schaffensprozess in das Bild, Farbmaterial kann sogar ins andere Farbfeld tropfen, an den Übergängen überlappen unregelmäßig die Farben; trocken oder auch in dichten Farbwellen.

Wie japanisch bzw. wie westlich ist diese Malauffassung? In welche Traditionen stellt sich Elvira Lantenhammer hiermit und wo kann man sie mit diesem Werk verorten? Schauen wir dazu kurz auf ihren künstlerischen Werdegang.

Sie hat eine solide handwerkliche Ausbildung als Restauratorin genossen und den Umgang mit Pigmenten, Bindern und Lösungsmitteln auch während ihres Studiums an der Akademie und später als freie Malerin weiterentwickelt und perfektioniert. Viele ihrer Bilder baut sie aus zahlreichen Schichten auf und teilt sie meist in geometrische Flächen auf. Häufig fällt hier der Begriff Farbfeldmalerei, eine abstrakte Richtung, die sich durch großflächige, homogen gefüllte Farbfelder auszeichnet. Sie ist laut Enzyklopädie weniger durch gestische Pinselstriche gekennzeichnet als durch die Gesamtbeschaffenheit von Form und Prozess. Definitionen von Kunstrichtungen sind wohl immer unscharf, wenn man sie auf die einzelne Künstlerpersönlichkeit anwendet. - Wie beschrieben, ist sich Elvira Lantenhammer sehr wohl der Bedeutung der Geste im Pinselstrich bewusst.

Aufmerksamkeit auf die Materialbeschaffenheit mit allen ihren kleinen gewollten Imperfektionen, das Einbringen des Subjekts in die Malerei, Atmen und Fließen in jedem Strich - sind dies nicht Charakteristika, die man auch mit japanischer Ästhetik und Zen in Verbindung bringen kann? Viele

They are parallel like the strokes of a rake, but straight. They do not have to react to stone settings as in her earlier pictures of Zen gardens.

On the scroll there is room for smaller imperfections and things similar to nature: slight folds in the paper bring traces of the creative process into the picture, color material can even drip into the other color field, at the transitions the colors irregularly overlap dryly or also in dense color waves.

How Japanese, or how western, is this painting concept? What traditions does Elvira Lantenhammer place herself in and where can she be located with this work? Let's take a brief look at her artistic career.

She enjoyed a solid craft apprenticeship as a restorer and developed and perfected the handling of pigments, binders and solvents during her studies at the academy and later as a freelance painter. She constructs many of her paintings from numerous layers and divides them mostly into geometric surfaces. The term color field painting is often used here, an abstract direction char-acterized by large, homogeneously filled color fields. According to the encyclopedia, it is less characterized by gestural brushstrokes than by the overall nature of form and process. Definitions of art movements are probably always blurred when they are applied to individual artists. - As described above, Elvira Lantenhammer is well aware of the significance of gesture in the brushstroke.

Attention to the nature of the material with all its small intentional imperfections, the introduction of the subject into painting, breathing and flowing in every stroke - are these not characteristics that can also be associated with Japanese aesthetics and Zen? Many

japanische Kunstrichtungen in den letzten tausend Jahren wurden von Zen beeinflusst, insbesondere die Philosophie von der Akzeptanz und Kontemplation der Unvollkommenheit, vom ständigen Fließen und der Impermanenz aller Dinge. Im 16. Jahrhundert wurde für diese von mir nur sehr oberflächlich beschriebene Ästhetik [vom Teemeister Sen no Rikyū] der Begriff „Wabi-Sabi" eingeführt. Deren Merkmale sind u.a. Asymmetrie, Rauheit, Schlichtheit, Bescheidenheit und Ruhe. Die Objekte haben häufig kleinere Makel oder Anomalien, die sich aus dem Konstruktionsprozess ergeben und dem Objekt Einzigartigkeit und Eleganz verleihen. Hinzu kommt eine Schönheit oder Gelassenheit, die mit dem Alter oder dem Gebrauch einhergeht. Vieles dieser ihnen sicherlich nicht ganz unbekannten Kriterien kann man an Elvira Lantenhammers Malerei und dem Kakemono festmachen. – Mit der Frische der Materialien und der Künstlichkeit der Farben kommt ein eher untypisches Element mit hinein. Letzteres wird allerdings durch die kraftvoll ausgewogenen Setzungen der Malerei, in denen die menschliche Hand zu spüren ist, aufs Beste ausgeglichen.

Das Rollbild kann zum Teil eingerollt präsentiert werden. Dies macht uns bewusst, dass ein eingerolltes Bild geheimnisvoll sein kann, weil es Teile verbirgt und dadurch interessanter erscheint. Dieses Rollbild braucht Weite – es wirkt aber auch, wenn nur ein Teil zu sehen ist, dann erfährt man es allerdings auf andere Art und Weise. Obwohl man die Gelegenheit hat, im Abschreiten das gesamte Rollbild zu lesen, ist man doch eher geneigt, mit Abstand den Gesamteindruck auf sich wirken zu lassen. Bei Ausschnitten ist man hingegen eher geneigt, sich auf Details und die einzelnen Abschnitte zu konzentrieren.

Japanese art movements in the last thousand years have been influenced by Zen, especially the philosophy of accepting and contemplating imperfection, the constant flow and impermanence of all things. In the 16th century, the term "Wabi-Sabi" was introduced by Sen no Rikyū for this aesthetic, which I described only superficially. Their characteristics include asymmetry, roughness, simplicity, modesty and calm. The objects often have minor imperfections or anomalies that result from the construction process and give the object uniqueness and elegance. In addition, there is a beauty or serenity associated with age or use. Many of these certainly not entirely unknown criteria can be traced back to Elvira Lantenhammer's painting and the Kakemono. – With the freshness of the materials and the artificiality of the colors, a rather atypical element comes into play. The latter, however, is well compensated by the powerfully balanced settings of the painting, where the human hand can be felt.

The scroll painting can be partly presented rolled up. This makes us aware that a rolled-up picture can be mysterious because it hides parts and thus appears more interesting. This scroll picture needs width – but it also works when only a part can be seen, but then you experience it in a different way. Although one has the opportunity to read the whole scroll while walking along it, one is more inclined to let the overall impression have an effect on oneself. With sections, on the other hand, one is more inclined to concentrate on details and the individual parts.

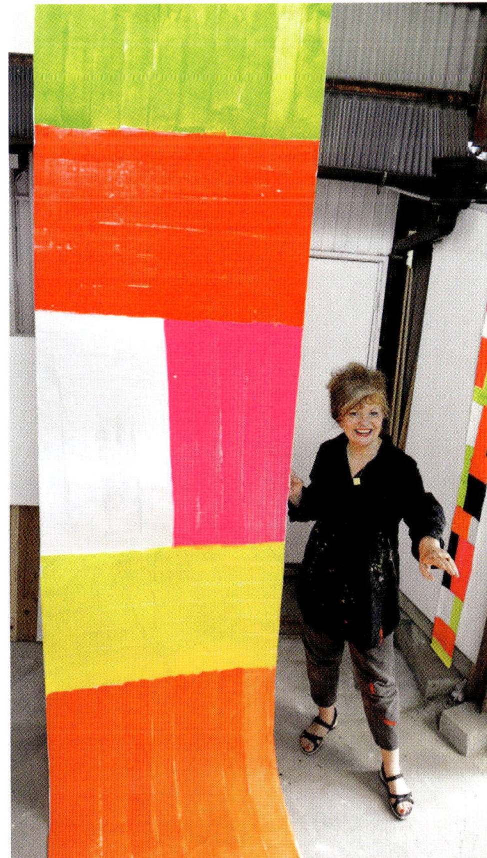

Studio Kura
Itoshima, Japan, 2017

## Kakemono

Bilderrolle in der Nische,
Tokonoma, des traditionellen
japanischen Hauses
aufgerollt, zur Aufbewahrung,
ist alles verborgen,
es kann nur teilweise entrollt sein,
nicht alles ist sichtbar,
birgt Geheimnis

Kakemono - Japanese Siteplan, 2017
Acrylics | Pigment | Shōji-paper
472.4 x 39.4 in. | 1200 x 100 cm

## Kakemono

Picture scroll in the alcove,
Tokonoma, of the traditional
Japanese house,
rolled up, for storage,
everything is hidden,
it can only be partially unrolled,
not everything is visible,
holds secret

Kakemono - Japanese Siteplan, 2017
Acrylics | Pigment | Shōji-paper
Detail

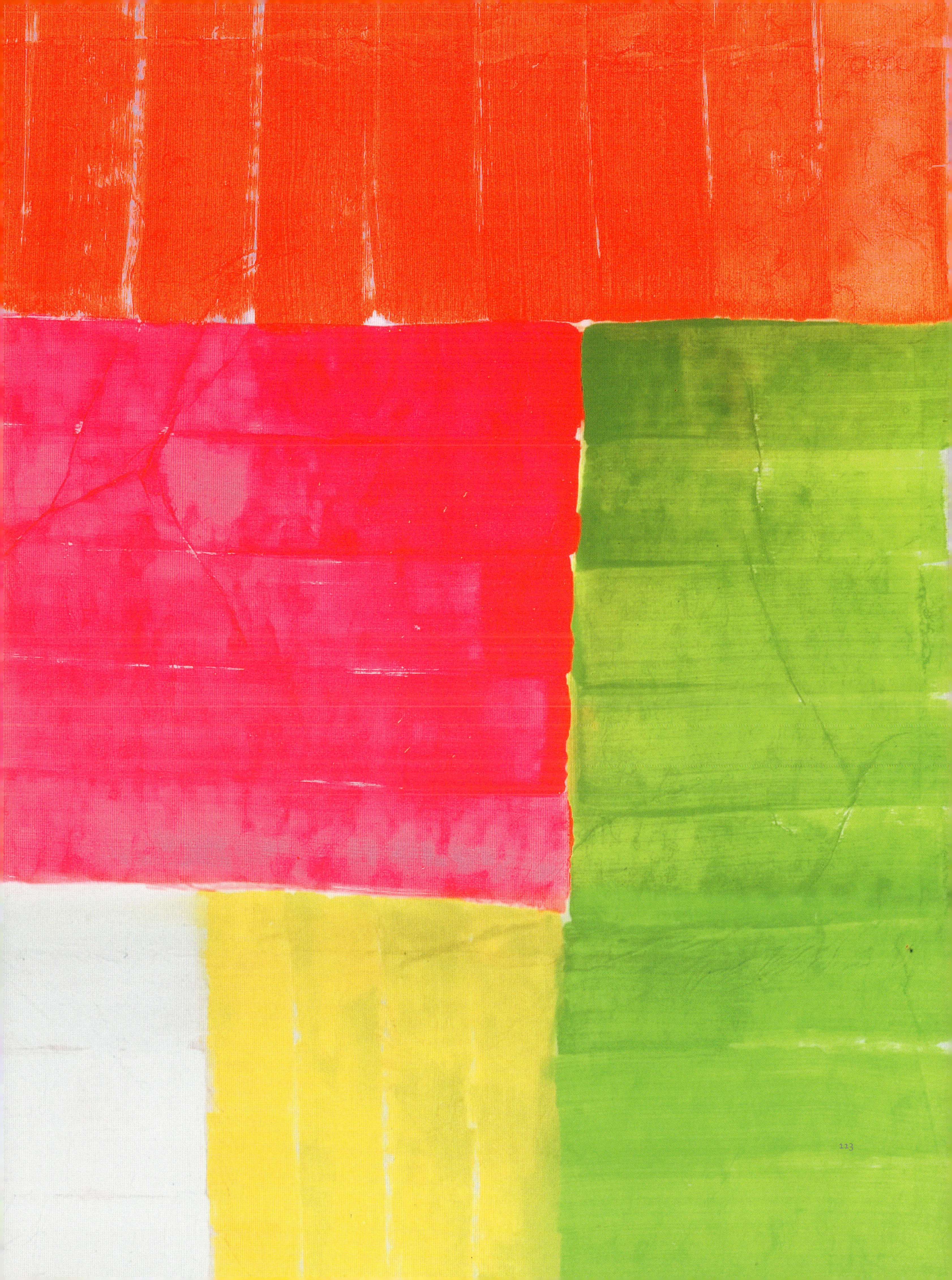

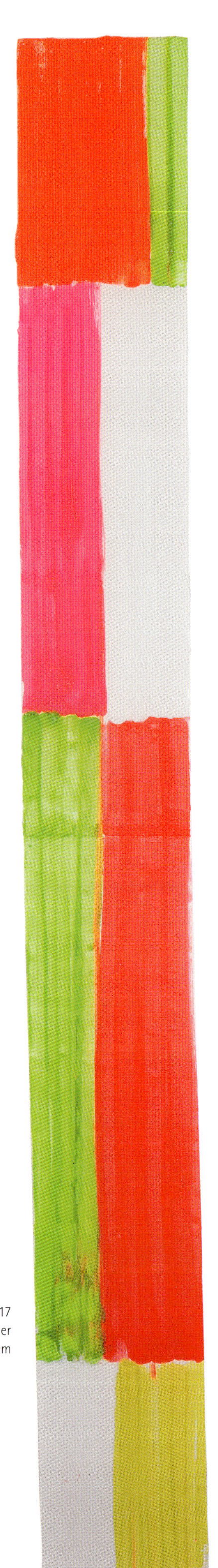

Kakemono - Japanese Siteplan, 2017
Acrylics | Pigment | Shōji-paper
47.2 x 11.8 in. | 120 x 30 cm

Kakemono - Japanese Siteplan, 2017
Acrylics | Pigment | Shōji-paper
47.2 x 11.8 in. | 120 x 30 cm

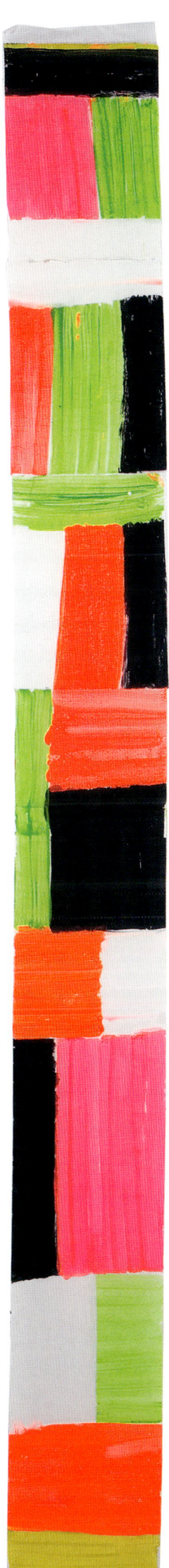

Kakemono - Japanese Siteplan, 2017
Acrylics | Pigment | Shōji-paper
55.1 x 11.8 in. | 140 x 30 cm

Kakemono - Japanese Siteplan, 2017
Acrylics | Pigment | Shōji-paper
35.4 x 11.8 in. | 90 x 30 cm

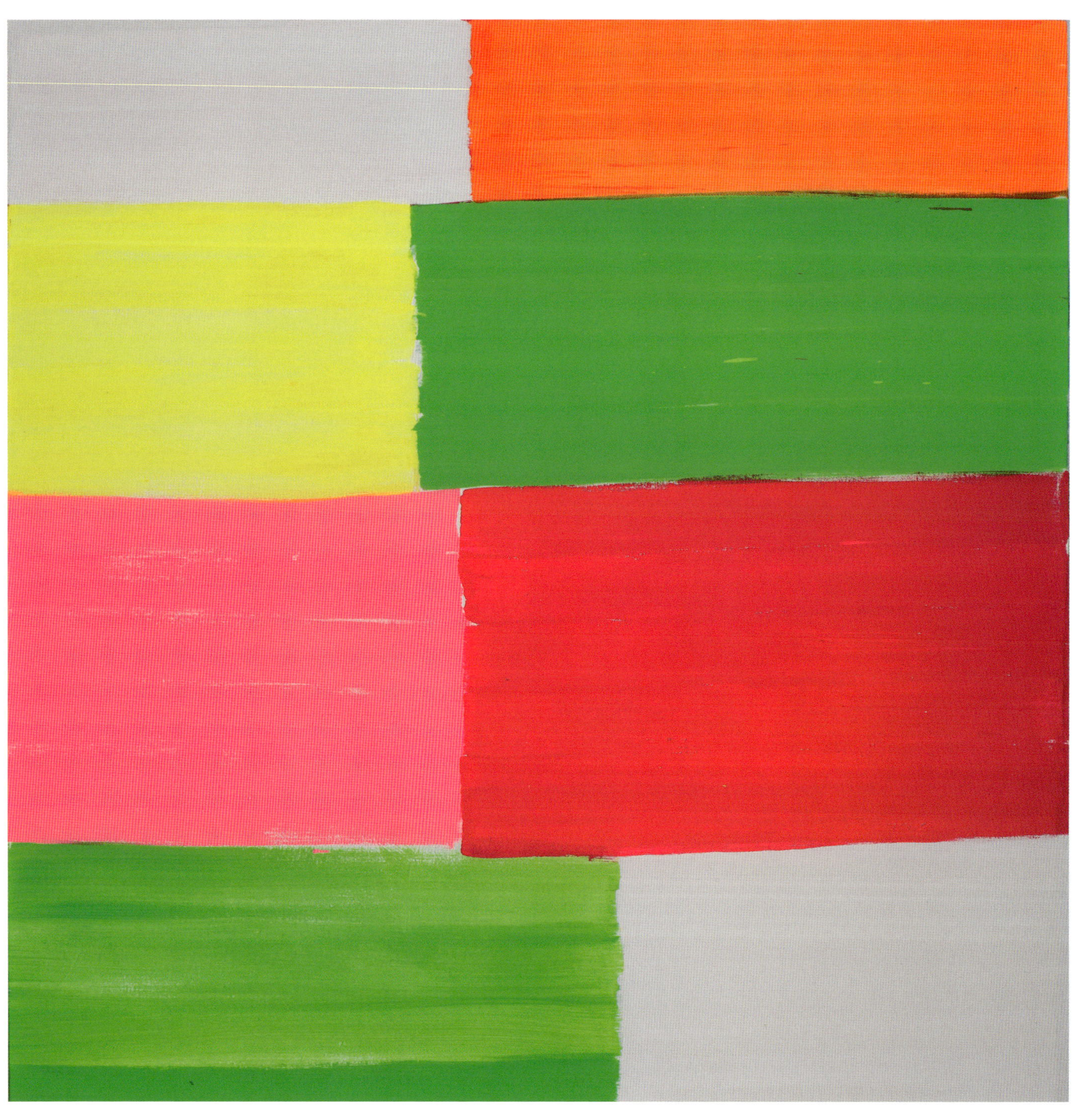

Japanese Siteplan, 2018
Acrylics | Pigment | Canvas
74.8 x 63 in. | 190 x 160 cm
Public collection

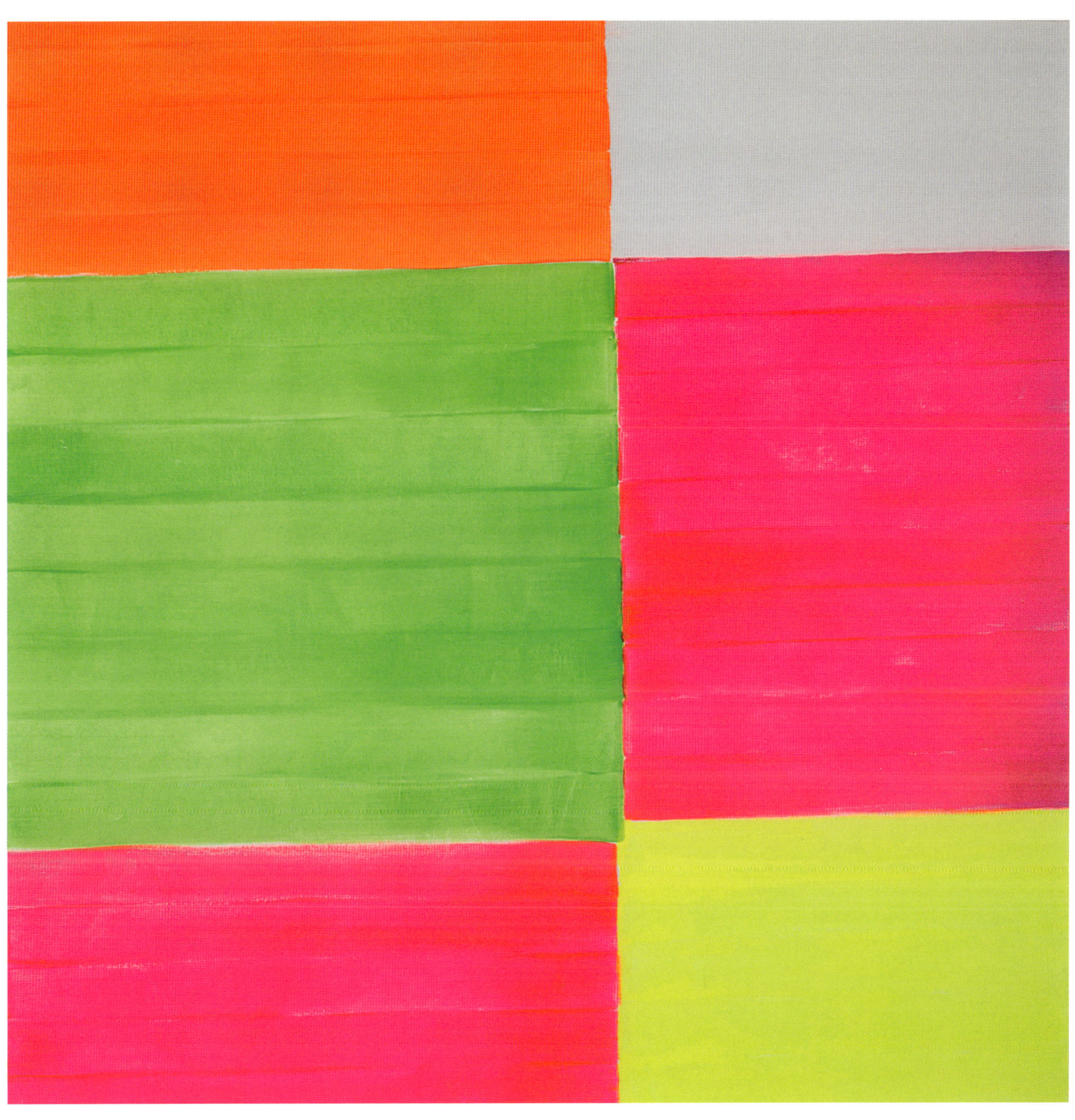

Japanese Siteplan, 2019
Acrylics | Pigment | Canvas
74.8 x 63 in. | 190 x 160 cm

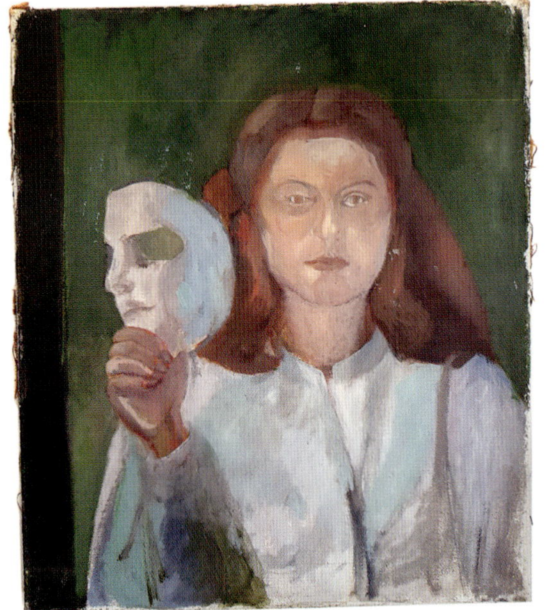

Dies feine, frühe Selbstbildnis mit gelüfteter Maske entbirgt nicht nur das Antlitz der jungen Künstlerin, zugleich manifestiert sich hierin, jenseits der Maske und eingespannt zwischen oberen und unteren Bildrand, eine in Schichten durchlässig gemalte, sich nach unten abdunkelnde Vertikale tiefgründigen Grüns. Aus diesem eher schmalen, gleichwohl bildprägenden vertikalen Feld, zusammen mit dem frei in helleren Grünstufen gemalten Fond vermeint man allerdings bereits untrüglich – regelrecht wie in einer Prophezeiung – den spezifischen Klang der Farbfeldmalerei ihres späteren Œuvres herauszuhören. Liegt die Ursache jeglichen schöpferischen Handelns doch in der Zukunft, da die Künstlerin, der Künstler im besten Falle etwas hervorzubringen in der Lage ist, was es so noch nie zuvor gegeben hat. Jene Befähigung zur Umkehrung der Ursache-Wirkungs-Richtung auf dem Zeitband ist Charakteristikum von KUNST.

U We Claus

This fine, early self-portrait with lifted mask reveals not only the face of the young artist, but at the same time, beyond the mask and held between the upper and lower edges of the picture, a vertical of deep green manifests itself, painted diaphanously in layers and darkening downwards. However, from this rather narrow vertical field, which nevertheless shapes the picture, together with the background freely painted in lighter green tones, one already seems to unmistakably hear – practically as in a prophecy – the specific sound of the color field painting of her later oeuvre. The source of all creative action lies in the future, since the artist, in the best case scenario, is able to produce something that has never existed before. That ability to reverse the cause-and-effect direction on the time band is a characteristic of ART.

U We Claus

# Elvira Lantenhammer

**Biografie**

| | |
|---|---|
| 1956 | geboren in Altötting |
| 1976 - 1979 | Ausbildung bei Restaurator Martin Zunhamer |
| 1980 - 1986 | Studium der Malerei an der Akademie der Bildenden Künste, München |
| seit 1998 | Initiatorin von Kunst in Schloss Homburg, Kuratorin lebt und arbeitet in Schloss Homburg am Main |

**Biography**

| | |
|---|---|
| 1956 | born in Altötting |
| 1976 - 1979 | Apprenticeship with restorer Martin Zunhamer |
| 1980 - 1986 | Art student at Akademie der Bildenden Künste, Munich |
| seit 1998 | Initiator of "Kunst in Schloss Homburg" and the "Sommerakademie Schloss Homburg," Curator lives and works in Schloss Homburg am Main |

**Auszeichnungen**

| | |
|---|---|
| 1994 | Debütantenpreis des Bayerischen Staates für Wissenschaft, Forschung und Kunst |
| 2000 - 2001 | Atelierstipendium des Bayerischen Staates |
| 2008 | Projektförderung aus dem Kulturfonds des Bayerischen Staates |
| seit 2010 | Mitglied im Deutschen Künstlerbund |
| 2011 | Kulturfonds des Bayerischen Staates |
| 2013 | Paul Ernst Wilke Stipendium |
| 2014 | Artist-in-residence Bulgarien-Stipendium des Kulturamts München |
| 2015 | Residency Virginia Center for the Creative Arts, Virginia, USA |
| 2017 | Artist-in-residence, Bharuch, Lecture Universität Baroda, Indien Artist-in-residence, artist's exchange, Fukuoka, Otsu, Japan-Stipendium der Stadt Würzburg |

**Awards**

| | |
|---|---|
| 1994 | Debut prize of the Bavarian State for Science, Research and Art |
| 2000 - 2001 | Studio-scholarship of the Bavarian State |
| 2008 | Project grant by the Culture Fund of the Bavarian State |
| since 2010 | Member of Deutscher Künstlerbund |
| 2011 | Culture Fund of the Bavarian State |
| 2013 | Paul-Ernst-Wilke Grant, Bremerhaven |
| 2014 | Artist-in-residence Bulgaria, by the Kulturamt München |
| 2015 | Residency Virginia Center for the Creative Arts, Virginia, USA |
| 2017 | Artist-in-residence, Bharuch, Lecture University Baroda, Gujarat, India Artist-in-residence Studio Kura, Itoshima, Prefecture Fukuoka, Japan Artist's exchange Otsu, Japan |

**Einzelausstellungen | Auswahl**
**Solo Exhibition | Selection**

2019 • *COLOR SITEPLAN*, BOK Offenbach
• *Farbenplan*, Galerie DeutschOrdensSchloss, Münnerstadt
• *LAGEPLAN*, Galerie Franck Haus, Marktheidenfeld
2018 • *Kakemono – Japanese Siteplan*, Siebold Museum Würzburg
2017 • *Kakemono – Japanese Siteplan*, Window Gallery, Seian University, Otsu, Japan
2016 • *Lagepläne*, ABC Westside Galerie, München
• *Siteplans*, Kunstverein Bayreuth
• *Virginian Siteplans*, Kunstverein Würzburg
2015 • *siteplan Bulgaria*, Galerie GEDOK , München
• *siteplan Bulgaria*, Galerie concrete cologne, Köln
• *Lagepläne* – Elvira Lantenhammer, Arbeitnehmerkammer Bremerhaven
2014 • *Siteplans Bulgaria*, Sofia Press Gallery, Sofia, Bulgarien
2013 • *Lageplan Bremerhaven*, Wilke Atelier, Bremerhaven
• *Lageplan Atlantis*, Rom und Central Park – Industrie und Kunst, ZF Friedrichshafen, Schweinfurt
2012 • *orange zu grau und andere Lagepläne*, Galerie Klaus Braun, Stuttgart
2011 • *Lagepläne – by heart!* Galerie Kunstreich, Bern, Schweiz
• *Die Essenz des Ortes*, Galerie Schwanitz, Würzburg
• *Offene Lage mit Schrein*, Stadtgalerie Altötting (C)
2010 • *Lageplan als Energie in Farbe*, Benediktushof, Holzkirchen
• *Turm II, Aussicht auf Vergnügen*, Galerie Pack of Patches, Jena
2008 • *Vom Antlitz der Orte*, Galerie Kunstraum 12, Ettlingen
• *... malen sichert vor tod und gefahr*, Galerie der Sparkasse Mainfranken, Würzburg
2007 • *Malerei, Plastik, Installation*, Gertrude Elvira Lantenhammer, Galerie der Bayerischen Landesbank, München (C)
2006 • *Lagepläne*, Bayer. Staatsministerium für Sozialordnung, Familie und Frauen, München
• *show it again...*, Neuer Kunstverein Aschaffenburg
• *Japanische Steinesetzungen*, Benediktushof, Holzkirchen
2005 • Zimmer-Galerie, C.P. Schneider, Frankfurt am Main
2004 • *Köpfe*, Galerie Stachowitz. München
• *Köpfe*, Schloss Homburg
2003 • *Köpfe* zu „... meine angenehmste Unterhaltung", Mainfränkisches Museum Würzburg (C)
• Schloss Schönfeld, Kassel
2002 • *nach innen offen*, Installation im Klinkersilo, HeidelbergCement, Lengfurt
2001 • Haus 10, Kloster Fürstenfeld
2000 • *Im japanischen Garten*, Galerie Ohm, München
• *Lagepläne*, IHK, Würzburg
1999 • *Kyoto*, Schloss Homburg
• *Atlantis - Kyoto - München – Venedig, Lagepläne*, Liebenweinturm, Burghausen
1998 • *Lagepläne Atlantis*, Goethe – Institut, München
• *Lagepläne*, Galerie Paleo, Köln
• *Lagepläne Würzburg - München – Venedig*, Orangerie, München
1997 • VDMA, Frankfurt am Main
• *Lagepläne*, Zimmer-Galerie, C.P. Schneider, Frankfurt am Main
1996 • Galerie des KVD, Dachau
• Galerie im Gang, Bamberg
1995 • *Eingekreist*, Produzentengalerie, Kassel
• Galerie im Bürgerhaus, Schwabach
1994 • Debütanten-Ausstellung, '94, Spitäle, Würzburg (C)

**Gruppenausstellungen | Auswahl**
**Group Exhibition | Selection**

2020 • *Augsburg Contemporary*
2019 • *sixty nifty*, Augsburg Contemporary
• *Kunst in den Mai*, GEDOK Galerie, München
2018 • *Domestic Space*, Domagk Edition, Halle 50, München
• *Black box(es)*, Saarländisches Künstlerhaus, Saarbrücken
• *Domestic Space*, Schloss Homburg Edition, Homburg am Main
• *Domestic Space*, Munich Edition, Zweigstelle Berlin, Artshop
• *abgefahren*, Else 2, Bahnhof Münnerstadt
• *Möbius-Schleife*, mit Kathrin Rabenort, Stadtgalerie Bad Soden
2017 • *Edition*, Portfolio Zweigstelle Berlin, Neue Galerie Landshut
• *Raum(er)greifend / Unruhe – Ordnung*, Galerie Basement, Wien, Österreich
• *Theurer Lantenhammer*, Plastik, Malerei, Spitäle, Würzburg
• *Black box(es)*, Faux Mouvement Centre d'Art Contemporain, Metz, Frankreich
• *Japanese Siteplans*, Elvira Lantenhammer, Gallery Studio Kura, Itoshima, Präfektur Fukuoka, Japan
• *summer saunter*, Galerie Klaus Braun, Stuttgart
2016 • *Lichte Masse*, mit Gunther Gerlach, Villa Sponte, Bremen
• *Farblagen* - Elvira Lantenhammer und Gerhard Scharnhorst, Galerie Klaus Braun Stuttgart

- *Similarities and Differences*, Viridian Artists Gallery, New York, USA

2015
- *beweglich = grün ohne Boden*, GEDOK München im Kunstverein Ebersberg
- *Arbeiten auf Papier*, Galerie Klaus Braun, Stuttgart
- *Virginian Siteplan*, VCCA, Virginia, USA

2014
- *Idea(s)*, Viridian Artists Gallery, New York, USA
- *Gold ton*, mit Karin Nedela, Galerie Zement, Frankfurt am Main
- *Lage mit Durchblick*, mit Manfred Emmen-Egger, Galerie Jutta Idelmann, Gelsenkirchen
- *Künstler auf Reisen*, IHK Würzburg

2013
- *Once Upon A Time*, Viridian Artists Gallery, New York City, USA
- *Affiliates - Disconnected Realities*, Viridian Artists Gallery, New York City, USA
- *art Karlsruhe*, vertreten von der Galerie Jutta Idelmann, Gelsenkirchen

2012
- *Endings and Beginnings*, Viridian Gallery, New York, USA
- 50 Jahre Städtepartnerschaft Würzburg-Caen, Wachsaal, Abteikirche St. Etienne, Caen, Frankreich
- *Schön - eine Bilderauswahl*, Galerie Klaus Braun, Stuttgart
- *gespräche in marrakesch*, Hotel Riad Honey, Marrakesch, Marokko
- *logbuch 2011*, Galerie Pack of Patches, Jena

2011
- *c.a.r.* Contemporary art ruhr, Essen
- Sudoh Gallery, Odawara, Japan
- Akademie für Politische Bildung, Tutzing
- Kunstmesse Karlsruhe

2010
- *cutlog*, Internationale Kunstmesse, Bourse du Commerce, Paris, Frankreich
- *versammelt*, BBK-Galerie, Museum im Kulturspeicher, Würzburg
- kunst zürich 2010, Internationale Kunstmesse, Zürich, Schweiz

2009
- *Kleine Lagepläne*, Palazzo Ducale, Genua, Italien
- *Kunst am Bau*, BBK-Galerie Museum Kulturspeicher, Würzburg (C)
- *Innerei*, IHK Würzburg-Schweinfurt

2008
- *mainseits*, Schloss Homburg am Main (C)
- *Blaubart*, bbk-Galerie, Kullturspeicher Würzburg (C)

2007
- *innerei*, Künstlerforum, Bonn (C)

2005
- Banque LBLUX, Luxemburg, (C)
- *Heimspiel*, Museum Kulturspeicher, Würzburg (C)

2003
- Kunstagentur Melchior, (mit Masaaki Maruyama) Kassel

(C) Catalog

**Arbeiten in öffentlichem Besitz, in öffentlichen Sammlungen und Kunst am Bau**
**Works in public ownership, permanent collections, and percent for art**

Sammlung / Collection Banque LBLux, Luxemburg
Neue Pinakothek, München / Munich
Museum im Kulturspeicher, Würzburg
Museum im Schloss Aschaffenburg
Bayerisches Staatsministerium für Sozialordnung, Familie und Frauen, München / Munich
Klinikum Main-Spessart, Marktheidenfeld
Fachhochschule Würzburg
Fachhochschule Ansbach
Fachhochschule Schweinfurt
Industrie- und Handelskammer / Chamber of Trade and Industry, Würzburg
LGA Würzburg
Landratsamt Dachau
Bund Deutscher Psychologen, Bonn
Justizvollzugsanstalt Würzburg
Staatliches Hochbauamt Würzburg
Stadt Altötting
Stadt Burghausen
Finanzamt Bad Kissingen
Bayerische Landesanstalt für Wein- und Gartenbau, Würzburg
Verband Deutscher Maschinen- und Anlagenbauer, Frankfurt am Main
Bereitschaftspolizei, Würzburg
Vermessungsamt Aschaffenburg
Finanzamt Aschaffenburg
ZIM Würzburg
OCEAN Working Building, Bremerhaven
Otsu City Hall, Otsu, Japan

IMPRESSUM
Colophon

Herausgeber / Editor: Galerie Zweigstelle Berlin, Andreas Stucken

Idee und Konzeption / Idea and concept: Elvira Lantenhammer

Autoren / Authors:
Hanneke Heinemann,
freie Kunsthistorikerin, Kuratorin
Henrike Holsing,
Kuratorin, Museum im Kulturspeicher Würzburg
Wolfgang Hülsen,
ehemaliger Vorsitzender des Kunstvereins Würzburg
U We Claus,
Board of Directors FIU Amsterdam.

Übersetzung / Translation: Karin Nedela

Lektorat / Copy-editing: Katrin Boskamp-Priever, Bremen

Gestaltung / Design: lutz: design, Würzburg

Fotografie / Photography: Anja Behrens, Sara Förster, Kathrin Heyer, Thomas Kohnle, Stefanie Scherbel, Ingo Peters

Projektleitung Verlag / Project management: Jürgen Kleidt

Verlag / Publisher:
Hirmer Verlag GmbH
Bayerstrasse 57-59
80335 München

Lithografie / Lithography: Reproline Genceller GmbH & Co. KG, München

Druck und Bindung / Printing and Binding: Printer Trento S.r.l., Trento
Printed in Italy

Papier / Paper: Gardamatt Art 150 g/m$^2$





ISBN 978-3-7774-3519-0
www.hirmerverlag.de
www.hirmerpublishers.com

Bibliografische Information der Deutschen Nationalbibliothek
Die Deutsche Nationalbibliothek verzeichnet diese Publikation in der Deutschen Nationalbibliografie; detaillierte bibliografische Daten sind im Internet über http://www.dnb.de abrufbar.
Bibliographic information published by the Deutsche Nationalbibliothek
The Deutsche Nationalbibliothek lists this publication in the Deutsche Nationalbibliografie; detailed bibliographic data is available on the Internet at http://www.dnb.de.

Mit großem Dank an / With many thanks: Raimund Mahlberg; Rita Freitag; Dorothea Freiin von Droste, Hotel am Main; Bernhard Kupsch

Unterstützt durch
Sponsored by

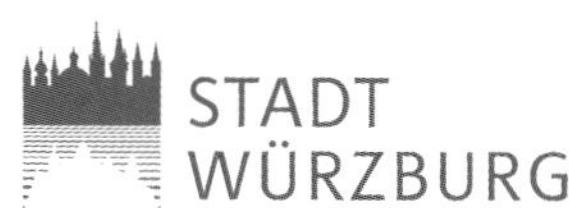


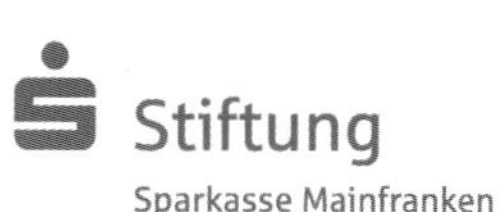


HEIDELBERGCEMENT